Hidden Messages

Hidden Messages

Instructional Materials for Investigating Culture

Barbara Finkelstein and
Elizabeth K. Eder, editors

INTERCULTURAL PRESS, INC.

For information, contact:
Intercultural Press, Inc.
P.O. Box 700
Yarmouth, Maine 04096 USA
207-846-5168

Book design and production by Patty J. Topel
Cover design by Patty J. Topel

Printed in the United State of America

02 01 00 99 98 1 2 3 4 5

Library of Congress Cataloging-in-Publication Data

Hidden messages: instructional materials for investigating culture / Barbara Finkelstein and Elizabeth K. Eder, editors.
p. cm.
Includes bibliographical references.
ISBN 1-877864-56-0
1. Multicultural education—United States—Audio-visual aids. 2. Multicultural education—United States—Curricula. 3. Culture-Study and teaching—United States—Audio-visual aids. 4. Language and culture—United States—Audio-visual aids. I. Finkelstein, Barbara, 1937- . II. Eder, Elizabeth K.
LC1099.3.H53 1998
370.117'0973—dc21 98-10404
CIP

Table of Contents

Acknowledgments

This book has been many years in the making. It has involved close collaborations between university staff at the International Center for the Study of Education Policy and Human Values at the University of Maryland, College Park, and an array of extraordinarily talented scholars, teachers, and cultural resource people in Japan, the United States, Puerto Rico, and El Salvador. By combining the efforts of theoreticians, practitioners, scholars, and teachers of diverse talents and cultural dispositions, we have, we hope, achieved innovative approaches to the study of culture in school.

As this book evolved, many individuals shared their wealth of knowledge and experience. Elizabeth K. Eder would like to express her appreciation to Barbara Finkelstein—scholar, mentor, adviser, and friend, who serves as professor and director of the International Center for the Study of Education Policy and Human Values in the College of Education at the University of Maryland, College Park; Sarah Pickert, professor of education at Catholic University, for her critical readings of the chapter; and Douglas Barry, former associate professor at the University of Alaska, Anchorage, for his keen insights and unfailing support.

Nancy Traubitz would like to thank her colleagues at Springbrook High School, Silver Spring, Maryland, especially principal Donald Kress and her students, who asked the questions that made her thinking, writing, and research possible.

Alan Chalk would like to thank Barbara Finkelstein for making his National Intercultural Education Leadership Institute (NIELI) trip to Japan possible, and Kathleen Woods Masalski, program director of the New England Program for Teaching about Japan, for sponsoring another research trip.

Corrine Mantle-Bromley wishes to thank the many language teachers in Idaho and Kansas who used and evaluated the lessons in her chapter in their various stages of development.

For their expert assistance and encouragement throughout the project, we would like to thank David Hoopes, editor-in-chief, and Judy Carl-Hendrick, managing editor, of Intercultural Press. Without their editorial and educational work, the lessons would be less than they are now—less useful, less lucid, and less friendly.

None of this would have been possible without the sustaining support of the United States-Japan Foundation and its dedicated staff—Stephen Bosworth, Ronald Aqua, Thomas Foran, and Hiroko Bloch. We are grateful for the quality and quantity of their support for this initiative.

Permissions

Grateful acknowledgment is made to the authors and publishers who granted permission to reprint the following selections:

1941-1991 Tora! Toyota! Cartoon by Wayne Stayskal. Copyright © 1991. Reprinted with permission of *Tampa Tribune.*

"Americans on Japan: It's a Love-Hate Thing." Copyright © 1991 ASM Communications Inc. Reprinted with permission of *ADWeek* magazine.

Chapter 9 from *Black Boy* by Richard Wright. Copyright © 1937, 1942, 1944, 1945 by Richard Wright. Copyright renewed 1973 by Ellen Wright. Reprinted with permission of HarperCollins Publishers, Inc.

"Crazy Distinctions in Bias Survey." Copyright © 1991 *Kansas City Star.* Reprinted with permission of Hispanic Link News Service, Washington, D.C.

Excerpts from *The River with No Bridge* by Sue Sumii, translanted by Susan Wilkinson. Copyright © 1989. Reprinted with permission of Charles E. Tuttle Company, Inc., Rutland, Vermont and Tokyo, Japan.

Excerpts from *The House on Mango Street* by Sandra Cisneros. Copyright © 1984. Published by Alfred A. Knopf, a division of Random House, Inc., New York, in 1994. Reprinted with permission of Susan Bergholz Literary Services, New York. All rights reserved.

Introduction

This book presents four conceptually sound, practical, user-friendly instructional units that we hope teachers will find particularly helpful as they seek to integrate cultural content into their curriculum; cultivate cultural sensitivity among their students; and add to the fund of cultural knowledge, skill, and understanding that students have available to make sense of the world, its people, and its possibilities.

The four instructional units comprise field-tested materials that have successfully helped middle school and high school teachers incorporate multicultural perspectives into traditional classes: history, geography, social studies, world culture, literature, language arts, foreign language studies, and performing and studio arts curricula. Because the units promote inquisitiveness and respect for alternative cultural habits and expressions, they have also been successfully integrated into diversity training programs for teachers and conflict-resolution initiatives for students.

Each of the following units is organized by instructional genre rather than by academic content or theme, thus making it possible for teachers to apply the units across disciplines and subspecialties and in a variety of instructional contexts.

Chapter 1, "Seeing the Invisible: Exploring Culture through Objects," will help students to become object-literate, an especially important enterprise in a world in which encounters between people of different nations, regions, and cultures will often occur without access to each other or each other's culture via language. Indeed, in today's global village, where more people of greater diversity interact without a shared language, the capacity to "read" a culture through its artifacts acquires particular salience. This unit focuses on the many ways to read an object to discover aspects of culture. It provides learning opportunities that will help students reflect on their own cultural conditioning and discover how it defines what they see and how they see it. It will prepare them *to attend to the context within which objects are created and used.*

Chapter 2, "Seeing through Words: Autobiography and Autobiographical Fiction as Vehicles for Cultural Understanding," focuses on the utility of works of autobiographical fiction and diaries to reveal culture, enhance the reading and writing capacities of students, foster sensitivity, and cultivate a sense of the capricious nature of justice and fair play. Through evocations of African American, Japanese, and Latino minority group life, it provides a foundation for students *to compare and contrast the meaning of minority in three cultures, to explore forms of discrimination,* and *to analyze the effects and processes of cultural labeling and dehumanization.* Lessons in name calling, the uses of language to dehumanize, and the phenomenon of racial isolation are all explored.

Proceeding on an assumption that cultural images are also significantly shaped and revealed through film as well as through objects and literature, chapter 3, "Seeing through Images: Cultural Learning through Film," explores the *use of film as a perspective-revealing vehicle* as well as a documentary resource for the study of history and how it is interpreted via the current national narrative. "Seeing through Images" invites teachers and students to investigate the medium of film as a history-making genre, exploring how film can shape collective memory, construct and deconstruct enemy images, define insiders and outsiders, and otherwise help students form a sense of nation and place. The chapter reveals ways to discover how filmmakers shape and reflect history through the imagery that they use, the stories that they tell, and the portraits of heroes and heroines that they draw.

Specifically, the unit calls on students to explore the films *December 7th* and *Tora! Tora! Tora!* and to reexamine and reinterpret historical events—here, the bombing of Pearl Harbor—from different national and cultural points of view, and to analyze the stories nations tell themselves as they go to war, cultivate peace, and seek reconciliation with former enemies.

Chapter 4, "Seeing through Language: Preparing Second or Foreign Language Learners to Explore Culture," engages students in explorations of cultural phenomena in advance of or in tandem with the study of foreign languages. The unit provides opportunities for them to consider the meaning of culture, discover stereotypes, recognize ethnocentricity, ferret out alternative cultural perspectives, cultivate their powers to observe and to suspend judgment, and otherwise attend to the complexities of culture. The unit provides an array of opportunities for students to *compare cultures, respond to cultural dilemmas, reflect on their own cultural repertoires, and decode culturally laden incidents.*

When taken singly or together, the contents of the instructional units inspire students to examine the cultural myths with which they make sense of the world, analyze the quality of information they receive about another culture, and become aware of the cultural filters through which information is shaped and cultural images are formed.

Each unit has a specific theme which integrates cultural content, employs a different medium (objects, literature, film, and language), combines cultural and academic study, and is adaptable across subject-matter specialties. Each unit contains learning objectives, materials required, procedures, activities, assignments, and other helpful information about how to present the content. In addition, each unit includes evaluation instruments that will assist teachers in determining attitude change as well as in assessing knowledge gained. Finally, each unit includes a reference list including new, primary, and other wonderfully useful but little-known resources for teachers.

As they present and interpret the history or geography text, autobiographical fiction, film, objects, or foreign language materials, teachers help shape students' reactions to cultural "others," bringing forth images of unfamiliar peoples and cultures and otherwise cultivating in their students a sense of place and community. No matter where or whom they teach, teachers in the twenty-first century will continue to function as cultural message carriers and, increasingly, as multicultural educators.

This book is designed to help them with the task.

1

Seeing the Invisible: Exploring Culture through Objects

Elizabeth K. Eder

Introduction

All too much learning is like a net full of insects. Some teachers have collected numbers, dates, lists of famous people, lists of events in their net. But to children, the world does not look like that. When their eyes explore the world, they see happenings, people, and things acting upon each other.[1]

This chapter is designed to help educators teach themselves, their students, and their colleagues how to use objects to explore nations and cultures in their classrooms. It will also assist educators in preparing culturally sensitive, object-based instructional materials that invite students to engage their senses in an effort to understand the worldviews, values, and aesthetic and expressive forms through which culture is revealed. As we shall see, the focus on objects enables teachers and students to approach the study of other cultures and peoples in stimulating, innovative, experiential, and learner-centered ways.

Through a systematic, carefully focused, and critical study of the physical characteristics of an object, students can learn to make inferences and judgments about the maker and/or owner of the object; the culture that produced the object; and the distinctive values, beliefs, and ways of knowing that give it life, meaning, and form.

Done well, teaching with objects can excite curiosity and help students become active participants in their own learning. It can facilitate the development of their perceptual and visual literacy skills. It can enable them to become less certain that they know the "truth" from the surface expressions of culture and to reflect critically on their own cultural assumptions, prejudices, and beliefs. It can enable them to think and work independently and to question intelligently. And finally, it can lead students to become aware of the follies of overgeneralization and the problems of subjective cultural interpretation and evaluation.

---

[1] Rudolf Arnheim, "Learning by Looking and Thinking," *Educational Horizons* 71, no. 2 (Winter 1993): 94-95.

Perhaps more than reading, writing, memorizing, drawing, singing, or composing, the study of objects can captivate students of all ages, backgrounds, and abilities. It can appeal to students who possess different learning styles and cultural and linguistic dispositions. As David G. Menser has suggested, "[object learning] brings a third-dimension reality to the classroom."[2]

The approach to object-based learning taken in this chapter can be used to teach about any culture, and the examples included throughout the text use several cultures to illustrate the principles and practices of effective object teaching and learning. This approach is based on the assumption that students already have a clear understanding of the concept of culture, that they can distinguish subcultures within a culture, and that they understand how they formed their own ideas about culture. If students need to review these concepts, you may wish to precede the lessons in this chapter with some of those described in chapter 4.

The Use of Objects

Objects are an inherent and important part of every culture, so deeply imprinted that we name Western historical/cultural periods after the kinds of material from which objects were produced in that era, for example, the Bronze and Iron Ages.

The analytical framework for this chapter is drawn from the discipline of anthropology, where objects are understood to be one part of a complex whole including "...artifacts, beliefs, art, and the other habits acquired by man as a member of society, and all products of human activity as determined by these habits."[3]

Most of the time objects, like other cultural artifacts such as books, films, and so on, reveal cultural values and beliefs only upon critical examination. They possess a tremendous power to educate, but their meanings may be invisible, silent, or misleading. According to one scholar,

> *A close examination of any object [constitutes] a graphic description of the level of intelligence, manual dexterity, and artistic comprehension of the civilization that produced it. It can reflect, as well, the climate, religious beliefs, form of government, the natural materials at hand, the structure of commerce, and the extent of man's scientific and emotional sophistication.*[4]

In fact the objects which we encounter on a daily basis are loaded with symbolic, economic, political, spiritual, and social meanings of which we are often unaware. For example, a national flag hanging in a classroom can be regarded as

---

[2] David G. Menser, "Ideas and Objects: The Artifact Kit," *Social Education* 30, no. 5 (May 1966): 343.

[3] Clyde Kluckhohn and W. H. Kelly, "The Concept of Culture," in *The Science of Man in the World Crisis*, edited by Ralph Linton (New York: Columbia University Press, 1945), 78-106.

[4] R. Latham, as quoted in Thomas J. Schlereth, *Artifacts and the American Past* (Nashville: American Association for State and Local History, 1980), frontispiece.

a piece of cloth, a patriotic object, a colorful decoration, a symbol of loyalty, an object of worship, the occasion for a song, or a concept around which children in school and citizens of a nation can unite. Needless to say, we may be aware of all of these meanings, but they are often outside our consciousness. Only rarely do we recognize that objects are cultural products, historically grounded and produced, and often unrecognizable to someone outside. In fact, some anthropologists, like Edward T. Hall, look upon objects as reflections of the hidden dimension of culture, "those common, unstated experiences which members of a given culture share [and] communicate without knowing...."[5]

Indeed, objects are more often than not removed from their culture or place in space and time. This fact leads some scholars to define objects as voiceless, yet often misleading. "The problem with things is that they are dumb.... And if by some ventriloquism they seem to speak, they lie.... Once removed from the continuity of everyday uses in time and space..., objects are transformed in the meanings that they may be said to carry...."[6] Because objects cannot speak for themselves, students need to be aware of not only what objects can tell them about culture, but what they don't tell them as well. As the French artist Henri Matisse said, "The effort needed to see things without distortion takes something very like courage."

Cultural Reflection through Object Teaching

Engaging in the process of object-based teaching and learning is not simple, neither for teachers nor students. For teachers, effective object-based teaching means a removal from center stage, a leave-taking of the role of knowledge transmitter and fact checker to that of perspective maker and critical reflector. Students, for their part, will need to become active seekers and critics, sensitive to and aware of the deeply complex and culturally loaded activity of looking at and gaining meaning from objects. They will have to cultivate self-reflective capabilities along with an awareness of their own cultural conditioning.

Seeing the invisible, obscure, or misleading will be a challenge as we learn to interpret objects based on our own cultural norms, which may include ethnocentric assumptions, cultural biases, and stereotypes. In order to transcend these, students will need to develop what anthropologists call an *emic perspective*, one which enables us to look at the physical world in terms of the categories used by the people who live in that world. Through a carefully guided examination of objects, students can learn to connect their own experiences and ways of knowing to those of others. They can, by a suspension of cultural identity, if only for a moment in time, learn to dwell in the experience of others and see the invisible.

---

5 Edward T. Hall, *The Hidden Dimension* (1966; reprint, New York: Anchor/Doubleday, 1982), x.

6 Spencer R. Crew and James E. Sims, "Locating Authenticity: Fragments of a Dialogue," in *Exhibiting Culture: The Poetics and Politics of Museum Display*, edited by Ivan Karp and Steven D. Lavine (Washington, DC, and London: Smithsonian Institution Press, 1991), 159.

The Practice of Object-Based Teaching

This section on the practice of object-based teaching will describe several approaches to teaching through objects. Since object collections don't often come prepackaged, the latter part of this chapter (pages 25–27) will suggest ways for educators to make their own object collections and will touch on selection criteria, methods of collection, and storage possibilities.

Successful object-based teaching is a sequential process which begins by developing students' capacity for critical observation. Although we use our sense of touch in early infancy to understand our surroundings, we are not often provided with a structured opportunity to further develop this skill later on. As a result, even though objects are part of our everyday experience, we may not be taught how to "read" an object as we are taught how to read a book, since the development of language abilities—reading, writing, and speaking—often takes precedence. One way to remedy this is to teach visual literacy skills (i.e., reading objects) in the classroom. Rudolf Arnheim, an expert in the psychology of art, calls this process "learning by looking and thinking."[7]

Competence in visual literacy requires the ability to use one's senses contemplatively, analytically, and selectively to identify and describe the formal elements of an object. These include its composition, design, shape, color, texture, size, mass, material, structural details, markings, and so forth. These elements are perceived immediately through our senses, and we can capture them through writing, drawing, speaking, or other means. Lesson 1 is designed to develop these skills by encouraging students to slow down, focus, and look critically and carefully at a familiar object. The lesson and its follow-up activity illustrate how objects, in this case a common paper clip and then a Styrofoam cup, can be used to enhance students' power of observation, to enable them to generate new perspectives, and to lead their thinking in many interesting directions.

Once students have gained basic visual literacy skills, they are ready to learn how to identify and then factually describe certain aspects of an object based on a model developed by historian E. McClung Fleming.[8] In lesson 2, students will follow Fleming's three-step model of identification: (1) classify, (2) authenticate, and then (3) describe an object. In doing so, students will examine every detail of an object, learn to make inferences about its authenticity, and prepare a detailed written description of the object that can be referred to later.

The first step in identification, classification, begins by asking "What is it?" However, even this simple question can be answered in a variety of ways. For example, when answering a question about what a "chop" is (used by the Chinese and others like a signature for official correspondence), one may respond

---

[7] Arnheim, "Learning by Looking and Thinking," 94.

[8] For additional information about Fleming's model see E. McClung Fleming, "Artifact Study: A Proposed Model," in *Material Culture Studies in America*, compiled and edited by Thomas J. Schlereth (Nashville, TN: American Association for State and Local History, 1982), 162-73.

based on function (a marker), material (a piece of stone), use (to seal documents), and so forth. The next step in identification is to determine whether the object is authentic. Questions raised might be "Is that the chop used by Mr. Chow?" "Is the chop made of plastic or is it really jade?" Authentification may be difficult for students to ascertain without extensive experience in examining and comparing objects; therefore, assistance from the teacher or an outside expert may be necessary. The final step in identification is description. This often provides information about the object's physical appearance. For example, the chop might be briefly described in the following manner: it is a rectangular-shaped, green, stone object about three inches tall and one-half inch wide, with red lettering carved on one end and a three-dimensional, lionlike animal carved on the other.

After learning how to identify an object based on Fleming's model, lesson 3 will greatly enhance students' understanding by engaging them in the task of learning how to evaluate objects in terms of the value standards of a specific culture. The difference between identification and evaluation is that the former tends to treat each object almost as if it were unique, whereas evaluation separates objects on the basis of dissimilar characteristics. This assumes that one object is compared with others of its kind (e.g., those made by the same individual, those made by different individuals within the same culture, and those from the same geographical region, etc.) and that there are historical or functional relationships among objects being evaluated.

In this lesson, evaluation of objects will be demonstrated in two ways. First, students will discuss the difference between subjective and objective value judgments and then apply this knowledge while playing a game that ranks objects based on students' individual value judgments. In the process, students will refine their perceptions, learn to examine their own responses and preconceptions (which will be different for each, since they will involve personal, conscious, and unconscious thoughts and feelings), and realize that whether they knew it or not, they have always separated and then ranked objects based on aesthetic qualities, levels of workmanship, and other factors in order to make the judgments they did. Second, students will learn to make factual comparisons between one object and others of its kind in quantifiable terms. Students will determine qualities such as size, cost, rarity, and so on through direct observation and outside research if necessary.

Next, after honing their visual literacy skills, engaging in identification and description, and learning two methods of evaluation, students can begin to explore objects through a consideration of their cultural context in lesson 4. The purpose of cultural analysis is to make inferences of a general nature about the culture that produced and/or used the object being studied. Therefore, cultural analysis goes beyond direct observation and visceral responses. It may reveal the object's functions in society (e.g., utility; conveyor of status, values, ideas, etc.), its historical significance, and the relationship of the object to the culture it comes from. For example, in this lesson students can learn to make inferences about where and when the object was made, by whom, for whom, and why. They can discuss what materials the object is made of, how the object was made, what techniques of construction were employed, and so on. They can also consider the possible roles and use(s) of the object in the culture that produced it. For example, if students look at a coin, such as a U.S. quarter, they may notice that a profile image of a man is on one side, along with the words "In God We Trust" and "Liberty." Based on these images and words students may infer that religion may play a role in this culture, that men may be revered individuals (e.g., heroes, gods, leaders, etc.), and that the people in this culture value freedom. The other side of the object features a bird with outstretched wings surrounded by a branch and an inscription in Latin, "E Pluribus Unum" (Out of Many One). Students may infer that the culture that produced this object values strength and that it has a diverse population. Students may also infer that the person(s) who made this object are technologically advanced because of the sophisticated workmanship (more than one type of metal is used). Although it is not easy to discover the culture behind an object, it can be accomplished through direct observation, background research, help from cultural informants, reference books, and other resources.

Whereas the activities in lesson 4 are concerned with the relationship of the object to its culture, the final lesson focuses on interpretation—the relationship between some fact learned about an object and some key aspect of our current value system. Students will draw some conclusions about the culture based on their findings and learn that there is never only one correct interpretation of an object, but many, depending upon the individual doing the interpreting. Because so much information will have been gathered by this point, an assessment or interpretation of the object in relationship to some key aspect of the culture can be made, but again this can only be inferred. For example, the function of a schoolbag in Japan (see Appendix A) is that of a container used by the elementary school student to transport books and other objects back and forth from school to home each day during the school year. However, the schoolbag also has a symbolic function in Japanese society. Often the bag is a gift from the parents or grandparents of the student before he or she begins formal education in first grade. This gift bears an important meaning for the student—now you are of the age to study very hard. In addition, although schoolbags are, for the most part, standard in size, shape, and color throughout Japan, the contents of each bag are different—the student can choose what type of pencil case, notepads, stickers, and so on to place inside. Therefore, the schoolbag not only creates a personal statement for the student but also provides important information about his or her place in society. Lesson 5 not only introduces students to aspects of interpretation; it also provides an opportunity to apply knowledge gained in the previous lessons in a culminating activity.

Using the Lessons

The lessons that follow were designed to be used with middle and high school students. Ideally, the concepts can be integrated into a broader context and therefore can be used at any point in the curriculum throughout the school year. While lessons may be suitable for many curricular areas and for other grade levels, some adaptation may be necessary.

Each lesson may be completed in one class session and lessons should be used sequentially whenever possible, since the concepts learned are meant to build on one another. However, these do not need to be taught in consecutive class periods. Keep in mind that the premise is to enable students to learn basic visual literacy skills and then apply those skills to (1) study the physical characteristics of an object, (2) make inferences about the maker and/or owner of the object, and (3) draw conclusions about the culture that produced the object based on the information learned and the characteristics observed.

Lesson 1–Observation

Objective: Students will

- examine a common object carefully and critically to determine its diverse physical characteristics
- write a detailed description based solely on visual evidence
- explain what can be learned from object study
- describe the skills necessary to learn from objects

Materials

- Six paper clips per student (This exercise can be done with any familiar object such as a pencil.)
- Egg timer or watch with a second hand
- Student notebooks

Procedure

1. Hand out one paper clip to each student. Ask the students to study the paper clip for one minute. When the minute is up, ask them to put the paper clip away and then quickly but as accurately as possible sketch the paper clip in a notebook (allow no more than two minutes). Students can then take the paper clip out again for a short discussion.
   - How does your drawing compare with the actual object?
   - What was difficult about drawing the paper clip accurately?
2. Ask students to describe a paper clip to someone who has never seen one before. Ask them to take turns giving a one-word description out loud (e.g., silver, shiny, etc.). No repeats are allowed (this may be a challenge!). Keep track of the words by writing them on the chalkboard. Next, ask the students to write a group description of the object. Encourage students to use words or phrases to describe the object based solely on what they see (e.g., silver), not on what they know (e.g., flexible). Ask a few students to read their descriptions out loud.
3. Hand out five more paper clips to each student and ask students to look at each one of them carefully for two to three minutes. Try to include both new and well-used paper clips. Have the students discuss their collection in small groups.
   - How are the paper clips similar? How are they different?
   - How do used paper clips compare with new ones?
4. Have students look at their collection of paper clips once again. Now, ask them to choose just one paper clip from the collection and write a description of it so that someone else will be able to find it in the group of six. After the descriptions are written, ask students to hand their

collection of paper clips and the description to a person sitting next to them to see if they can find the paper clip that was described.

Evaluation

Have students respond to the following after completing both activities in this lesson:

- What does the expression "a picture is worth a thousand words" mean?
- How does this expression apply to objects?
- What can we potentially learn when we look at an object?
- Name at least two skills that are required in order to learn from objects.

Lesson 1—Observation
Follow-up Activity[9]

Objective: Students will

- learn to look carefully and critically at a more complex object to increase their powers of observation

Materials

- One Styrofoam cup per student (This exercise can be done with other familiar objects, but a Styrofoam cup works particularly well, as do plastic six-pack rings.)

Procedure

1. Hand out one Styrofoam cup to each student. Ask the students to study the cup carefully for a few minutes without talking.
2. Lead a discussion about the cup. Throughout the discussion, limit students' responses to purely descriptive observations. Students' responses may stray toward interpretive or evaluative answers. If this is the case, you may want to discuss why it is sometimes difficult to describe an object or event objectively. (Experience indicates that this is an effective pattern for the discussion to follow.)
   - What is this?
   - How would you describe it?
   - Is there anything significant about its shape or color? (Try to elicit answers that include that it has no handles, it can be stacked, it is a graduated cylinder, etc.)
   - What else do you notice? (Try to elicit answers that include markings such as lines, bumps, letters, or symbols.)
   - Where (in what environments) have you seen this object?
   - Is there anything else you would like to add?

Evaluation

Ask students to write a description of the object for someone from another culture who may not be familiar with this kind of object. Remind students to limit their description to information they acquired through direct observation only.

---

[9] This exercise has been adapted from John Hennigar Shuh's "Teaching Yourself to Teach with Objects," *Journal of Education* 7, no. 4 (1982): 8-14.

Lesson 2—Object Study

Objective: Students will

- identify and describe objects using Fleming's three-step model of identification
- give examples of classification, authentication, and description
- prepare a detailed written description of the object that can be referred to later
- make inferences about an object's authenticity
- learn the difficulties of applying language to description

Materials

- A common object from a cultural group studied in the classroom
- One copy for each student of the Object Study Activity Sheet

Procedure

1. Explain Fleming's three-step process to students, using an object as an example. Be sure to remind them that this is one way to learn how to identify and describe objects.
2. Hand out one Object Study Activity Sheet to each student. Ask students to study the object for a few minutes before independently answering the questions on the activity sheet. Encourage them to look carefully at all of the dimensions of the object: its shape, structural details, markings, material, color, and so forth before beginning to write. Give them about ten minutes to fill out the activity sheet, then discuss student responses.

Evaluation

No more than one week after the lesson ask students to write a description of Fleming's three-step model of identification. Have them explain what they learned about object study when they applied this model.

Student Handout

Lesson 2—Object Study
Activity Sheet

1. Classification
   In order to answer the question "What is it?" describe the object in terms of
   a. function(s)

   b. material(s)

   c. use(s)

2. Authentication
   Do you think this object is authentic? Give your reasons.

3. Description
   Write a detailed description of the object.

Lesson 3—Evaluating Objects

Objective: Students will

- be able to identify two types of object evaluation: judgments and factual comparisons based on quantifiable terms
- differentiate between subjective and objective judgments
- practice stating their judgments about an object's characteristics
- examine their own responses and preconceptions when making judgments
- be able to separate and then rank objects based on an object's aesthetic qualities, level of workmanship, and other factors in order to make judgments

Materials

- Four or more objects from a culture studied in your classroom
- One set of five tokens per student. Cut the tokens out of cardboard or sturdy paper. The tokens should be approximately two inches in diameter. On each token draw one of the symbols listed below (or students may be asked to do this).

Procedure

1. Tell students that the purpose of this lesson and its follow-up activity is to evaluate objects in at least two ways: by making value judgments and by making factual comparisons of one object with others of its kind in quantifiable terms.
2. Ask students to define *judgment* in their own words.
3. Place a collection of four or more objects on a table. The objects should all be similar (e.g., all made by the same person or from the same geographic region) and all well documented (students should be able to research the artist, technique, geographic region, etc.) or different. Be sure to leave adequate space between and in front of the objects, as students will be placing tokens near them.
4. Hand out a set of tokens to each student. Explain the meaning of each token to them.

   Heart—the object you like the best

   $—the one you think costs the most

   Clock—the one you think took the longest to make

   Frame—the one you would most like in your home

   Heart with a slash through it—the one you like the least

5. Instruct students to look carefully at the objects and spend at least a minute thinking about where to place each token. Students can then go to the table of objects, individually or in groups, and place their tokens.
6. Assign one student per object to count the various tokens and record the totals on the board.
7. Lead a discussion about the students' choices, saving the object(s) that students liked the least until last. Ask students to name at least one thing that the maker of the unpopular object(s) did well.
8. Discuss the difference between subjective and objective judgments.
   - What is a subjective value judgment? (It is a preference that you *feel*, and it is justified by reasoning, aesthetic judgment, "gut feeling," etc.)
   - What are some examples of subjective value judgments that you made about the objects?
   - What is an objective judgment? (It is a preference based on objective criteria, what you *think.)*
   - What are some examples of objective judgments that you made about the objects?
   - Is making a subjective or objective judgment a simple or a complex act? Justify your answer.
   - Why are subjective judgments sometimes dangerous?
9. Ask students to examine their earlier definitions of *judgment* and their own responses and preconceptions. Discuss why these may be different for each individual.
10. Ask students why an understanding of subjective and objective judgments is important in object study.
11. Ask students to list the criteria (subjective and objective) that they used (perhaps unknowingly) to judge the objects in order to do the activity. List them on the board.

Evaluation

Ask students to describe in writing an example of a time they made a subjective evaluation about someone or something that turned out to be wrong. What were the consequences? Ask students to also describe a situation in which they made an objective judgment.

Lesson 3—Evaluating Objects Follow-up Activity

Objective: Students will

- make factual comparisons of one object with others of its kind in quantifiable terms

Materials

- Four or more objects from a culture studied in your classroom. (The same objects used in lesson 3 may be used again.) For each object you will need to write a list of quantifiable characteristics that students may use in writing their descriptions (number 3 below), but don't make this task too easy for them.

Procedure

1. Have students brainstorm about characteristics that could be used to classify an object with "others of its kind" (e.g., same or different maker, geographic region, culture, etc.). List the characteristics on the board.
2. Have students name quantifiable terms that can be used to evaluate an object (e.g., size, cost, rarity, material, technological innovation, association with a famous person, etc.). List the terms on the board.
3. Have students individually select one object from the group to study in depth. Ask them to write a complete, detailed description of the object based solely on visual evidence (see lesson 1). Students will now need to do additional research about the object to learn more about its maker, the technique used, the geographic area or culture, and so on in order to then make a factual comparison of the object with others of its kind using the quantifiable terms they came up with. Discuss their findings.

Evaluation

Conduct an in-class discussion about the two forms of evaluation and what type of information can be obtained about an object by using each method.

Lesson 4—Exploring Cultural Context

Objective: Students will

- define the term *inference*
- apply *inference* to the study of objects
- be able to explain why "seeing isn't always believing"

Materials

- One object per student (that each brings from home and keeps hidden in a brown paper bag)

Procedure

1. Ask students to bring in an object from home that they think best reflects something about themselves. Have them keep the object hidden in a brown paper bag. Ask students to each make a short list of the attributes their chosen object reflects about them that they expect their fellow classmates will discover. Ask students to exchange paper bags (objects) in pairs. Each student will take the object out of the bag, study it carefully, and then make a list of attributes that they think the object reflects about their fellow student. Ask the pairs to exchange attribute lists and discuss them.
2. Hold a discussion with the entire class. Use this group discussion as a jumping-off point for defining and talking about the term *inference* (to draw a conclusion or make a deduction based on evidence).
   - Did your partner interpret the object the way you thought he or she would? Why or why not?
   - Did she or he see things that surprised you? If so, what were they?
   - When you were making a list of attributes for your classmate's object, where did your knowledge of the object and your classmate come from?
3. Ask students to think about how seeing isn't always believing and give some examples of this (e.g., card tricks). How might this idea apply to the following quote from the French painter and sculptor Henri Matisse (1869-1954)?

> *To see is itself a creative operation, requiring an effort. Everything we see in our daily life is more or less distorted by acquired habits, and this is perhaps more evident in an age like ours when the cinema, posters, and magazines present us every day with a flood of ready-made images which are to the eyes what prejudices are to the mind. The effort needed to see things without distortion takes something very like courage.*

Evaluation

Have students respond to the following within a week of doing this exercise:

- Define inference.
- How does this term apply to object study?
- What are ready-made images and how are we bombarded by them every day?
- How might they affect our ability to "see"?
- What does Matisse mean when he says "ready-made images...are to the eyes what prejudices are to the mind"?
- Why is "learning to look" more difficult than it might seem?

Lesson 4—Exploring Cultural Context Follow-up Activity

Objective: Students will

- discuss the concept of culture and how they formed their ideas about it
- make inferences of a general nature about the society that produced and/or used an object being studied in the classroom
- examine objects through a consideration of their cultural context

Materials

- One object from the United States that students cannot easily identify (a kitchen gadget works well)
- One Exploring Cultural Context Activity Sheet per student

Procedure

1. Ask students to define some of the characteristics of U.S. culture. List them on the board.
2. Use the list as a springboard to talk about the concept of culture and subcultures within a culture (see chapter 4 for suggestions). This could lead to a discussion of how students formed their ideas about culture and how this may affect their ability to describe and draw conclusions about a culture.
3. Discuss how all objects have a function which can operate on several levels, for example, decorative, communicative (conveying status, ideas, values, feelings, meanings), technical (use), social, and so on. These elements can be explored to learn about how a particular object reflects the culture it comes from.
4. Hand out one Exploring Cultural Context Activity Sheet per student. Display the object so that all students can take a close look at it, but ask them not to discuss it out loud. Give students about ten minutes to independently answer the questions on the activity sheet.
5. Discuss student responses and then provide information about the object.

Evaluation

Have students answer the following questions within a week of doing this exercise:

- What can we know for sure about this culture by looking at this object?
- What can we infer about the culture?
- What can't we know without further study?
- How could you find out more about the object?
- Why might it be difficult to explore objects through a consideration of their cultural context?

Student Handout

Lesson 4—Exploring Cultural Context
Activity Sheet

1. Quickly sketch the object in the space below.

2. List six words (adjectives) that describe the object.

3. What is the object made of? List the material(s).

4. What do you think the object is/was used for?

5. What can you determine about the person(s) who made it?

6. What inferences can you make about the culture this object came from and why?

Lesson 5—Interpreting Meaning

Objective: Students will

- define *status symbol*
- discuss how status symbols reflect contemporary cultural values

Materials

- Three or four contemporary American magazines per small group of students
- One Interpreting Meaning Activity Sheet 1 per group

Procedure

1. Ask students what they think are the most important status symbols in U.S. culture today. List these symbols on the board. Discuss the following questions with students, then bring the discussion around to how these status symbols reflect aspects of our current value system.
   - How do these symbols confer status?
   - From where do these symbols originate?
   - Is price most important?
   - What (other) factors are involved?
2. Ask students to work in small groups. Ask each group to look at three or four contemporary American magazines and identify at least one automobile advertisement from each. One member from each group should record the group's answers to the questions on the activity sheet.
3. Ask each group to report their findings. Discuss how advertisements appeal to individual perceptions of at least one type of status (e.g., socioeconomic).

Evaluation

Have students respond to the following within a week of doing this exercise:

- Define *status symbol.*
- Discuss how status symbols reflect contemporary cultural values.
- List other primary or secondary sources that could be used to determine contemporary cultural values (e.g., a menu, a television commercial, etc.).

Student Handout

Lesson 5–Interpreting Meaning
Activity Sheet 1

Type of automobile: ______________________________

1. What words are used to convey status?

2. What images are used?

3. To whom is this ad directed (e.g., gender, age, income, race, etc.)? How do you know?

4. How does the ad appeal to people's perceptions of status?

Lesson 5—Interpreting Meaning Follow-up Activity 1

Objective: Students will

- define *interpretation*
- learn that there is never only one correct interpretation but many, depending upon who is doing the interpreting
- interpret an object to draw a relationship between some fact learned about the object and some key aspect of our current value system

Materials

- One object from the United States
- One object from a culture not studied in the classroom

Procedure

1. Discuss the following with students: What is an interpretation (e.g., the relation between facts learned about the object and some key aspects of our current value system)? How do we make interpretations? Where do we get the information to make interpretations from? Can an object be interpreted in more than one way? Why or why not?
2. Display an object from the United States that might be interpreted as valuable in contemporary culture because of a specific criterion (or set of criteria). Ask students to interpret the object based on this criterion. The importance of the object might therefore be interpreted as the fact that it is expensive, very old, difficult to obtain, and so on. Compare students' various interpretations, keeping in mind that there can be many correct interpretations.
3. Ask students to come up with a list of other factors that can be used to interpret an object (e.g., size, newness on the market, uniqueness, etc.). Write student responses on the board. Display the second object (from a culture not studied in the classroom) and ask students to interpret it based on one of the factors they just listed. Discuss their findings.

Evaluation

Have students respond to the following within a week of doing this exercise:

- Write a definition of *interpretation*.
- Explain the difference between an inference and an interpretation.
- List at least two factors that can be used to interpret an object.

Lesson 5—Interpreting Meaning Follow-up Activity 2

Objective: Students will

- apply knowledge gained in the previous lessons in order to review terms and concepts

Materials

- One object with multiple meanings (e.g., a Mexican or Japanese mask)
- One Interpreting Meaning Activity Sheet 2 per student

Procedure

1. Display the object and ask students to study it for one minute. When the minute is up, put the object out of sight and ask them to quickly sketch the object as accurately as possible (no more than two minutes). Take the object out again and ask students to compare their drawings with the object.
2. Hand out one activity sheet to each student. Ask students to study the object again before independently answering the questions on the activity sheet. Discuss student responses.

Evaluation

Ask students to complete the following tasks:

- Describe the three-step model of identification.
- Define the difference between subjective and objective value judgments.
- Describe how and why an individual in the next century might use this object to learn about some key aspects of current cultural values.

Student Handout

Lesson 5–Interpreting Meaning
Activity Sheet 2

1. Describe the object in terms of
   a. function(s)

   b. material(s)

   c. use(s)

2. Do you think this object is authentic? Give your reasons.

3. List six words (adjectives) to describe the object.

4. Fill in the blanks.
   a. This object is the most________________ of all the objects we have studied in class.
   b. This object is the least________________ of all the objects we have studied in class.
   c. Compared with other objects of its kind that we have seen in class, this object________________.

5. What is the object made of?

6. What do you think the object is/was used for?

7. What can you determine about the person(s) who made it?

8. Who may have owned it?

9. What inferences can you make about the culture this object came from and why?

10. Interpret the object based on one of the factors discussed in class. List the factor and describe the reason behind your interpretation.

Developing an Object Collection

Selecting Objects

One of the most important considerations in developing an object collection for use in the classroom is selection. Consider answering these kinds of questions for each object before it is added to a collection:

- What does the object illustrate?
- How does it fit into the lesson (or curriculum)? (If the object doesn't help to clarify or illustrate a point that you are trying to make, most likely it is not the correct object to use as an example.)
- What message does it convey?
- What aspects of culture does it reveal?
- What aspects of culture does it obscure?

No object should be thought of as autonomous or unconnected to other objects or to the individuals in the culture that produced it. Therefore, a diverse group of objects should be assembled to represent multiple facets of the life and culture your collection focuses on, rather than a particular view.

The next important consideration is whether the object is touchable. Try to select objects that can be used and handled without fear of damage. For example, a Japanese tea bowl, which was created to be held in the hand and admired by examining all its dimensions through sight and touch, would be an excellent choice. But if there is concern over its possible breakage, then its use as an object in the classroom may be limited.

Touchability brings to mind another consideration—that of authenticity. Whether an original, reproduction, or facsimile is used may depend on a number of factors including touchability, availability, replaceability, cost, and most important, the purpose you wish the object to serve. Whenever possible, it is usually desirable to use an authentic object. However, a particular object may be difficult to find, too expensive to purchase, or difficult to replace if it is damaged or broken. If this is the case, a reproduction (an object made to closely resemble the original), a facsimile (a close reproduction that may differ in scale), or a replica (an exact reproduction in all details) may be a desirable substitute. For example, a parchment manuscript from France is probably too fragile to handle on an ongoing basis; thus a facsimile made out of paper might be a better choice. However, when a facsimile or reproduction is used in place of the original, one should still be sensitive to the material the original object is made of and to its origin and use. For example, an object may look like a painted lacquer doll from Russia, but it may be made of plastic in a factory in another country and sold in Russia to tourists. To avoid any potential problems, check the object's authenticity to be certain of its use and origin. Whenever possible, seek advice from cultural informants, museum personnel, or perhaps from the foreign language or cultural studies department at a local college or university.

Collecting Objects

Objects from other countries have become increasingly available in the United States through a variety of sources. One convenient source may be a local food, department, or variety store. For example, almost any Japanese, Mexican, Italian, or Chinese food item or kitchen utensil can be used as either a starting point for discussion or as the basis for an entire lesson. Another source is in community organizations such as museums and historical societies. Many such institutions not only have gift shops but also mail-order catalogues filled with interesting objects. Be certain that the objects borrowed or purchased meet the criteria for selection mentioned above. The Internet, of course, is a virtual gold mine for locating objects and other resources. See Appendix B (pages 33–37) for some examples.

In addition, university resource centers as well as individuals may be useful sources for locating objects. For example, the Mid-Atlantic Region Japan-in-the-Schools (MARJiS) Program, located on the University of Maryland campus, maintains an extensive collection of objects from Japan in its resource center. Descriptions of a selection of objects from the MARJiS Resource Center are located in Appendix A (pages 28–32).

Individuals such as foreign students, immigrants, visiting businesspeople, and so on can serve as informal cultural "experts" in the classroom. They may be able to advise you on the selection, use, or authenticity of objects; know other individuals involved in community organizations who can assist in a variety of ways; or demonstrate or discuss objects in your school. Preferably, an informant should be a member of the culture he or she is representing. However, even though someone was born in a particular country, it does not mean that he or she is an expert in all aspects of life and culture there, especially if the individual has not lived there for some time. Therefore, it is important to invite several individuals to serve as cultural informants.

Another method of collecting objects is to purchase them in situ. The same criteria (selection considerations, touchability, and especially authenticity) should be kept in mind. Even if you have no plans to travel to the target culture, you may be able to locate someone who does. If so, whenever possible provide a detailed descriptive list of objects and possible places to purchase them. Cultural informants may be particularly helpful with this process. An additional source of objects is through an educational materials exchange program, which, though time-consuming, offers an exciting opportunity to make a connection with individuals from another culture. An educational materials exchange can be initiated when a member of the school staff meets a colleague from another culture at a conference or through a professional organization, when a student has been involved in a formal exchange program, when a parent is a member of a Sister City organization, through the advice of a cultural informant, or through contact made via the Internet, to name a few. Once a relationship is established, the actual process of exchanging objects is not complicated. A class or school from one culture assembles a collection of objects to share with a class or school in the target culture. Students on both sides of the exchange collectively decide which objects best represent a specific aspect or aspects of their culture and then, ideally, label and describe them, explaining why they chose each object. Students may also want to guess what types of objects they think they will be receiving, what these objects reflect about the other culture, and why they may have been selected. When the collection is received, the students can then examine their preconceptions and compare and contrast the objects with what they thought would be sent. In one recent case, two elementary schools—one in Tokyo, Japan, and one in a small town in southern Maryland—engaged in an educational materials exchange program. The principals began their cross-cultural exchange with a series of letters written over a period of several months. Through this correspondence the principals learned about their respective schools; they shared their personal and educational philosophies, dreams, and aspirations; and they experienced the challenges of cross-cultural communication, as letters needed to be translated in order to be read and enjoyed. The principals then decided that, in order to build stronger international awareness among their students, they would arrange an exchange of objects. In Maryland, the principal made the primary decisions about what to send, but she also asked some of the students to select objects. In the process, the students began to ask questions such as "Why does our school have a mascot and what does it mean?" "Does this plastic water bottle have a common meaning for the students in our class? the entire school? the United States?" "What aspect of our culture does this object (a school yearbook) represent?" "What types of objects will we get?" Through the principal's and teacher's leadership, students explored the meaning of culture, learned about the importance of symbols, and became aware of their own cultural biases and ethnocentric assumptions; in other words, they had a rich culture-learning experience.

Storing Your Collection

Along with the increased benefits of a collection also come concerns about the storage of objects. These include (but are not limited to) preservation, security, and space requirements. Particularly if you plan to lend your objects to other schools or community groups, portability becomes very important. One solution is to store objects in a lightweight, colorful box (preferably with handles) that can stack easily and safely and can double as a display and transport container. Within the box, the original objects should be protected as well. Commercial suppliers for high-quality storage materials are located in Appendix B.

Appendix A

Exploring Culture through Objects: Selections from the MARJiS Discovery Box, Elementary School Life in Japan

Introduction

The Mid-Atlantic Region Japan-in-the-Schools (MARJiS) Discovery Boxes[10] each contain a collection of thematically linked objects from Japan with related resources. The Discovery Box profiled below, Elementary School Life in Japan, attempts to bring the world of the elementary school student and classroom practices in Japan into view. All of the objects were actually used by elementary school students or teachers, and many were donated by a public elementary school in Tokyo.

Any object in this box can be used to teach about Japanese culture. Through a carefully guided examination, students will be able to identify and describe the formal elements of each object. They can then learn to make critical judgments about the objects which will enable them to explore their own reactions and preconceptions. Finally, students may want to learn about the objects' cultural context to draw some conclusions about the culture based on their findings.

Detailed descriptions and discussions of two objects in the Elementary School Life in Japan Discovery Box follow. A complete list of the contents of the Discovery Box is also included, with a brief description of each object and related resource. Use these examples as a departure point for thinking about how a similar description and analysis of the culture you are studying can be done in your classroom, be it elementary or secondary, so that students can learn to explore culture through objects.

Schoolbag

Preparations for the first day of elementary school in a Japanese child's life usually begin several months before school opens. These preparations may include becoming informed about safety issues, attending meetings held by the school for parents of entering children, and purchasing various school items such as a schoolbag, or *randoseru* (ran-doe-seh-roux).

---

[10] MARJiS Discovery Boxes are available on loan to teachers from Maryland, Virginia, West Virginia, and the District of Columbia. Contact: MARJiS Program, 3104 Benjamin Building, University of Maryland, College Park, MD 20742; 301-405-7350 (phone) or 301-405-3573 (fax).

All children in grades one through six in public elementary school use a *randoseru* to carry items back and forth from home to school each day during the school year. The bag is worn like a backpack so that the child's hands are free. Very often the schoolbag is a gift to the student from his or her parents or grandparents. This gift carries an important meaning to the student—now you are of the age to study very hard.

Throughout Japan, *randoseru* are generally standard in size, shape, and color. Boys usually carry a black bag and girls use a red one. However, though schoolbags look the same on the outside, each bag is personalized on the inside with the student's belongings such as a pencil case, notebooks, and so on. In addition to having one's name, grade, and class on the bag, some children decorate their bags on the inside with charms or stickers which reflect their individual interests.

Calligraphy Set

Historically, Japanese warriors and noblemen alike sought to be accomplished calligraphers, as mastery of the fundamentals of writing represented an attainment of character on the part of the practitioner and was believed to develop spiritual discipline. This respect for the art form is still found today; calligraphy is taught in a separate class period in upper elementary and lower secondary grades, and *shuji* (shoe-gee), the Japanese equivalent of penmanship, is taught in lower elementary grades.

The calligraphy set, which includes a red box, a blue box, various brushes, ink bottles, and other materials, is designed to be used in an elementary school classroom and contains all of the traditional calligraphy tools as well as a few modern ones (implements have changed little since the art form was first practiced in Japan). This kit contains the two basic kinds of brushes: thick and slender. The former is used mostly for the main body of writing and the latter is usually used for inscriptions, signatures, cursive-style writing, or fine work. The base of both styles of brush is made of bamboo and the tip, from animal hair. Ink is usually made from soot from a wood fire, mixed with glue, and formed into a stick (this is in the red box). Sticks are often decorated and can be quite elaborate in design. To make liquid ink, the ink stick is rubbed with a very small amount of water from the water dropper (in this case a clear plastic bottle) onto the ink stone (kept in the blue box). Water droppers are usually made of ceramic or metal and can be found in any shape. (Some kits may also contain a bottle of already prepared liquid ink, a container to store leftover liquid ink, a sponge, and/or lids for the brushes.)

MARJiS Discovery Box Contents

Objects

- Schoolbag*
- Lunch Box

  This plastic container is sometimes used by elementary school students in Japan to carry lunch to school. Although almost all public elementary schools offer school lunch services, lunch boxes are usually prepared with great care at home if a student is going on a field trip, participating in a special school event such as Sports Day, or if lunch is not served in school.

- Pencil Case

  This type of container is used by elementary school students to carry pencils, erasers, and other small desk supplies in their schoolbag. Pencil cases vary greatly in style and design and can therefore reflect the student's individuality.

- Student Essay

  This essay was written by a sixth-grade female student in Japan. It describes her feelings about having violated the class rule of exchanging money and therefore gives us insight into some of the classroom practices in her school and about student responsibilities. The teacher's supportive yet firm comments are also recorded on the essay.

- Note Page Protector

  Some students use a note page protector to create a hard surface for writing and to protect their papers. They can choose a protector with their favorite cartoon character, rock musician, or other design, which will reflect something of their interests and personality.

- Textbooks

  Japanese Language Textbook

  This textbook is the first of two Japanese language textbooks used by fourth-grade students during their school year. Textbooks are often small-sized paperbacks issued in two separate volumes so that they are lightweight and easy for students to carry back and forth from school to home each day in their schoolbags. Each chapter in this textbook introduces new words or characters in either a story or a poem. In this book alone, 129 new kanji *(Chinese characters) are introduced. Japanese language is a required course for all public school students in grades one through twelve.*

  Arithmetic Textbook

  This math textbook is also the first of two textbooks used by fourth-grade students. It covers geometry, division, graph reading, equations, and numbers higher than a hundred million. The book is used with an accompa-

* Starred objects have been described in more detail on the preceding pages.

nying drill book which reinforces skills learned in class and is used for homework assignments. Math is a required course for all public school students in grades one through twelve.

Science Textbook
This textbook is the first of two fourth-grade science textbooks and covers how to use a microscope and how to perform experiments using a potato, insects, water, and weights and scales. Science is a required course for all public school students in grades three through twelve.

Social Studies Textbook
Also the first of two textbooks, this social studies textbook is used by fourth-grade students during the school year. The book's theme is cooperation and the process of development. Social studies is a required course in grades three through twelve.

Moral Education Textbook
Our Ways, *a fourth-grade textbook, contains twenty-four stories, each with a different theme, which are meant to be used as a departure point for classroom discussion. Moral education is a required subject in grades one through nine.*

- School Lunch Menu
  This booklet was prepared by the nutritionist of an elementary school in Tokyo. It contains school lunch menus and copies of a newsletter prepared for students and their families. It shows the care with which this nutritionist planned meals and the high priority assigned to developing "sound minds and bodies."

- Lunch-Serving Uniform
  Very often lunch is served in the school and students take turns serving lunch in the classroom or cafeteria. This is one of the many ways that students learn about different roles and responsibilities. When students serve lunch they wear a special uniform, consisting of a hat and a jacket, designed just for that purpose. Each student is responsible for purchasing a uniform, which is stored in a special bag.

- Exercise Clothing
  Students are responsible for purchasing their own exercise clothing, which is used for physical education classes and Sports Day activities. Although often not standard in style, the uniform must be the correct color. Sometimes there is a separate uniform for summer and winter, and the boys' and girls' uniforms are slightly different. This is one of many ways that students are separated by gender during their elementary school years.

- Calligraphy Set*

- Math Set
  This is a supplementary classroom kit for first-graders and is designed to make math problems fun. If the teacher decides to use this type of learning aid in the classroom in addition to a textbook, then he or she would ask the students' parents to purchase a kit and label each one of its parts.

This is just one of the many ways that parents contribute to their child's education in a very hands-on manner.

- Abacus
  Even in an age of calculators and computers, the abacus, a traditional instrument for calculation, is still taught in many third- and fourth-grade math classes. Some researchers believe that training on the abacus increases the students' ability to calculate quickly in their heads and improves concentration as well.

- Origami Paper and Origami Examples
  Origami, the traditional art of folded paper, is still taught in many art classes in lower elementary school, as it has been since the turn of the century. The importance of origami is in the process, so it is introduced in the art curriculum to build students' skills at precision, accuracy, and persistence.

- Student Essays Booklet
  This booklet contains a collection of essays written on a wide variety of themes by fourth-grade students at a school in Tokyo. These essays reflect the hopes, dreams, frustrations, and delights of a group of elementary school students and provide important insights about classroom practices as well as school events.

- Brochure for Visitors to the School
  This brochure was written for visitors to an elementary school in Tokyo. It includes a history of the school, its goals, a description of research activities, school statistics, a floor plan, and the school song. This provides not only a blueprint of one school's priorities but reflects the Ministry of Education's concerns and policies as well.

- Newsletters for Parents
  This booklet contains a collection of newsletters which were written for parents by a second-grade teacher in Tokyo. The newsletters reflect the close working relationship between the teacher and his students' parents, his expectations for parent involvement, and his personal goals and aspirations for his students.

Appendix B

Selected Locations to Purchase Cultural Objects

The Art Institute of Chicago
111 South Michigan Avenue
Chicago, IL 60603-6110
800-621-9337 (gift catalogue requests)
Online catalogue: artic.edu/aic/shops/catalog.html
Offers gifts, jewelry, and museum adaptations from around the world.

The Cleveland Museum of Art, Museum Store
11150 East Boulevard
Cleveland, OH 44106
216-421-7340, extension 129
Online catalogue: clemusart.com/
A wide variety of objects is available.

Isabella Stewart Gardner Museum
2 Palace Road
Boston, MA 02115
617-566-1401
Museum shop sells reproductions from their collection, including jewelry and some crafts, mainly European.

Metropolitan Museum of Art
82nd Street and 5th Avenue
New York, NY 10028
212-879-5500, extension 4092 (North Shop)
Online catalogue: metmuseum.netcart.com/
Objects from all over the world, based on the museum's collection.

Museum of Fine Arts, Boston
PO Box 244
Avon, MA 02322-0244
800-225-5592
Online catalogue: mfa.org/shop/
Shop features jewelry, printed reproductions, decorative items, clothing for men and women, and educational toys based on works in the museum's collection. Catalogue is available.

National Gallery of Art Museum Shop
Constitution Avenue N.W. between 3rd and 7th Streets
Washington, DC 20001
800-697-9350
Online catalogue: nga.gov/shop/shop.htm
e-mail: mailorder@nga.gov
Gallery shops feature printed reproductions, stationery, and jewelry based on the museum's permanent collection and exhibitions.

Peabody Essex Museum
East India Square
Salem, MA 01970
978-745-1876, extension 3119
Online shop: pem.org/shop/default.htm
e-mail: shop@pem.org
Sells objects from around the world.

Seattle Art Museum
100 University Street
Seattle, WA 98101-2902
206-654-9100
Online catalogue: seattleartmuseum.org/
Wide range of objects from all over the globe.

Smithsonian Institution
National Mall
Washington, DC 20560
To request a catalogue: 800-322-0344
Online catalogue: si.edu/youandsi/products/start.htm
e-mail: sicustsvc@aol.com
Sells jewelry, clothing and accessories, toys, collectibles, decorative objects, books, music, videos, and more, based on the Smithsonian's vast collections.

Spertus Museum
618 S. Michigan Avenue
Chicago, IL 60605
312-322-1776
Website: spertus.edu/Museum.html
e-mail: sijs@spertus.edu
Rents "museum-in-a-box" kits with cultural artifacts and archival photographs on past and present aspects of Jewish culture. *Tools and Treasures of the Torah* includes a wooden *tik* and velvet *me'il.*

UCLA Fowler Museum of Cultural History
Family Programs/Education Department
Box 951549
Los Angeles, CA 90095-1549
310-206-5663
Museum shop sells publications, posters, prints, books, jewelry, and handcrafted works of art that center around current exhibitions.

Organizations and Commercial Distributors

Asia

Arise
6925 Willow Street, NW
Washington, DC 20012
202-291-0770
Website: arisedc.com/arise/index.html
e-mail: sales@arisedc.com
Warehouse of imports from Japan, China, Indonesia, and the Philippines. Limited online catalogue available. Baskets, kimonos, carvings, buddhas, stone lanterns, dolls, *yukatas*.

AskAsia
Website maintained by the Asia Society where teachers can obtain educational materials on Asian culture for K-12, including images.
Website: askasia.org

France

Cesar, Inc.
25 East 21st Street
8th Floor
New York, NY 10010-6293
Manufacturer, importer, distributor of masks, animal noses, armor, helmets, wigs, beards, moustaches, costumes, and accessories. Catalogue available.

Germany

Goethe Institute
Boston, MA: 617-262-6050
Los Angeles, CA: 213-525-3388
St. Louis, MO: 314-367-2452
Houston, TX: 713-528-2787
New York, NY: 212-439-8700
Washington, DC: 202-289-1200
Also in Ann Arbor, Atlanta, Chicago, San Francisco, Cincinnati, Seattle, Montreal, Vancouver, Toronto. Call for local sources of information and products.

Latin America

Chimayo Trading Company
13029 Ventura Boulevard
Studio City, CA 91604
818-783-0079
Website: venturablvd.com/chimayo_trading_co
e-mail: chimayo@venturablvd.com
Direct imports from Latin America, including ceramics, drums, beads, wood earrings, and an eclectic mix of traditional arts and crafts.

Russia

Volga River Trading Company
354 North Street
Burlington, VT 05401
802-863-6686
Wholesale and retail goods from Russia and Eastern Europe, including *matryoshka* (nesting dolls).

General

Aid to Artisans
14 Brick Walk Lane
Farmington, CT 06032
860-677-1649
e-mail: atausa@aol.com
Write or e-mail for a list of trade network members (producers of authentic crafts).

Christian Children's Fund
Global Crafts
500 Main Street
PO Box 518
New Windsor, MD 21776-0518
Write for catalogue of crafts and other products from foreign countries, including Ecuador, Russia, and Africa.

The Highsmith Company
West 5527 Highway 106
PO Box 800
Fort Atkinson, WI 53538
800-558-2110
Commercial supplier of high-quality storage materials.

Light Impressions Archival Supplies

439 Monroe Avenue
PO Box 940
Rochester, NY 14603
800-828-6216
Commercial supplier of high-quality archival storage materials.

Stanford Program on International and Cross-Cultural Education

Littlefield Center
Room 14
Stanford University
Stanford, CA 94305-5013
800-578-1114
Website: stanford.edu
Search for "K8 Catalog"
e-mail: Spice.Sales@forsythe.stanford.edu
Sells educational materials, mostly print and audiovisual. Online catalogue of materials on global issues, world culture, geography, history.

UNICEF

UNICEF House Gift Shop
3 UN Plaza
New York, NY 10017
212-759-0760
United Nations UNICEF Card and Gift Shop
Visitors Center, Lower Level
UN Plaza
New York, NY 10017
212-963-7696
Website: unicef.org/gco/gco.htm
Crafts and gifts from around the world. Write or visit their website for catalogue.

Selected Bibliography

Ames, Kenneth. "Introduction." In *The Colonial Revival in America,* edited by Alan Alexrod. Wilmington, DE: Henry Francis duPont Winterthur Museum, 1985.

Andersen, Janis F., and Robert Powell. "Intercultural Communication and the Classroom." In *Intercultural Communication: A Reader,* 6th ed., edited by Larry A. Samovar and Richard E. Porter. Belmont, CA: Wadsworth, 1991.

Arnheim, Rudolf. "Learning by Looking and Thinking." *Educational Horizons* 71, no. 2 (Winter 1993): 94-98.

Crew, Spencer R., and James E. Sims. "Locating Authenticity: Fragments of a Dialogue." In *Exhibiting Culture: The Poetics and Politics of Museum Display,* edited by Ivan Karp and Steven D. Lavine. Washington, DC, and London: Smithsonian Institution Press, 1991.

Deetz, James. "The Link from Object to Person to Concept." In *Museums, Adults, and the Humanities: A Guide for Educational Programming,* edited by Zipporah W. Collins. Washington, DC: American Association of Museums, 1981.

Fleming, E. McClung. "Artifact Study: A Proposed Model." In *Material Culture Studies in America,* compiled and edited by Thomas J. Schlereth. Nashville, TN: American Association for State and Local History, 1982.

Gardner, Howard. *Multiple Intelligences: The Theory in Practice.* New York: Basic Books, 1993.

Hall, Edward T. *The Hidden Dimension.* 1966; reprint, New York: Anchor/ Doubleday, 1982.

Kluckhohn, Clyde, and W. H. Kelly. "The Concept of Culture." In *The Science of Man in the World Crisis,* edited by Ralph Linton. New York: Columbia University Press, 1945: 78-106.

Menser, David G. "Ideas and Objects: The Artifact Kit." *Social Education* 30, no. 5 (May 1966): 343-45.

Schlereth, Thomas J. *Artifacts and the American Past.* Nashville, TN: American Association for State and Local History, 1980.

Shuh, John Hennigar. "Teaching Yourself to Teach with Objects." *Journal of Education* 7, no. 4 (1982): 8-14.

2

Seeing through Words: Autobiography and Autobiographical Fiction as Vehicles for Cultural Understanding

Barbara Finkelstein and Nancy Traubitz

Introduction

There are few types of literature that illuminate culture as poignantly or as provocatively as works of autobiography and autobiographical fiction. Through personal recollection and lived experience, writers of autobiography and autobiographical fiction give readers uncommonly powerful lenses through which to view their own experiences, communicate and share those experiences with others, and ultimately reflect on their own habits of heart, mind, and association. Works of autobiography and autobiographical fiction reveal the ways in which individuals experience the power of economic and political circumstance. They expose the ofttimes hidden dimensions of inhumanity by rendering the impersonal, personal; the abstract, concrete; the hidden, visible. They give personal meaning to abstract concepts like *prejudice* and *discrimination.** Like all diaries and fine works of fiction, autobiographies and works of autobiographical fiction enable readers to empathize with the emotions of others, view otherwise invisible miseries, imagine the intolerable, and, through identification with sympathetic others, learn to go beyond stereotypes to discover a common humanity. The genre provides a realistic context for students to discover the voices of cultural others; reflect on different ways of knowing, being, and doing; and, through this process, begin to substitute understanding for prejudice.

In this chapter, we invite teachers and students to study a particular form of autobiographical fiction, which we will call *narratives of oppression*—stories which writers have constructed to make sense of and reveal their lives as members of less-privileged minority and gender groups.

Narratives of oppression are not happy stories. They dramatize encounters between weak and strong, haves and have-nots, the privileged and the disadvantaged. They reveal the hurt, grief, rage, despair, and emotional cost of being members of less-privileged, unacceptable, pitied, and/or despised social groups. They reveal the darker side of diversity. But narratives of oppression do more than

* Throughout this chapter, we will distinguish between prejudice and discrimination by defining *prejudice* as a habit of mind and *discrimination* as an act of exclusion.

chronicle misery and degradation. Through the interpretive framework of their creators, they become vehicles through which the humanity and strength of cultural others become visible to readers. Through the stories that they tell, writers present their view of life as it is lived and experienced on the other side of the tracks or behind ghetto walls; they disclose the invisible social spaces where encounters with cultural others can reveal a human capacity to do good as well as evil, to elevate as well as degrade, to lend a helping hand as well as inflict pain and suffering.

If they are carefully studied and sensitively presented, narratives of oppression invite teachers and students to approach painful, unrecognized, unfortunate, and unattended tendencies of our common humanity: to label, demonize, and degrade those who are different; to deny the presence of discrimination, inequality, and injustice; to side with those who are powerful and to blame those who are weak for conditions which are often out of their control. These narratives can reveal the power of language to sustain conflict and/or to cultivate understanding between persons of differing social status, disparate racial and ethnic groups, and different genders. They reveal the power of language to do harm or to do good. They enable students to hear new voices, to revisit old ones, and to discover culture and in the process re-create it as well.

This chapter has been prepared for stouthearted teachers willing to lead students down a path of literary study that will bring them face-to-face with the experience of discrimination. It explores (1) how language becomes an instrument of discrimination through the use of words that defile, demonize, insult, segregate, label, and otherwise distance or do violence to cultural others, separating society into ingroups and outgroups, haves and have-nots, friends and enemies and (2) how autobiography and autobiographical fiction can be used as a particularly powerful medium to study the lives of people who experience discrimination.

This chapter centers on the study of two major narratives of oppression and several shorter ones. The first narrative of oppression, Richard Wright's *Black Boy,* reveals the workings of *racial discrimination* as it was experienced by a young African American in the American South in the 1920s. His intention was to dramatize the nature of "the culture from which [he] sprang...[and] the terror from which [he] fled."[1] He lived in the South at a time when racial segregation was legal and omnipresent, suffusing every aspect of daily life—the locations and conditions of living quarters, the schools that students attended, the busses they boarded, the seats they took, the water fountains from which they drank. He grew up in a place where the legacies of slavery were everywhere. Through the voice of the novel's protagonist, an intelligent, sensitive African American male growing up in the historical and geographical context of racial hatred and misogyny, and through the use of tough, angry, provocative prose, Wright creates a narrative of striking power.

---

[1] Richard Wright, *Black Boy: A Record of Childhood and Youth* (1945; reprint, New York: Harper & Brothers, 1993), 303.

The second narrative of oppression is an autobiographical novel by Sue Sumii entitled *The River with No Bridge* (*Hashi no nai kawa*), which documents the condition of oppression and self-hatred of a group of outcast Japanese. The subjects of the story, known as Burakumin or "village" (*Buraku*) "people" (*min*), experience a virulent form of discrimination which we are calling *status discrimination* in order to distinguish it from more familiar forms of discrimination. Burakumin are racially and linguistically indistinguishable from other Japanese. They speak Japanese, they look Japanese, but they have experienced an historical pattern of discrimination based on occupation, location, and place of origin. They live in a group society where equality is highly valued. Notwithstanding this belief and an equally strong commitment to status uniformity among Japanese people, this particular group of Japanese citizens has been historically cast out and considered polluted and dirty. They are what one writer has called an invisible minority, occupying a subordinate position, suffering from social disabilities, sharing a common identity, and living typically in segregated communities throughout Japan. Their experience is movingly portrayed through literary forms that are distinctively Japanese but are no less compelling as mirrors of cultural reality.

Two of the short selections that follow relate, through reminiscences by nonprofessional writers, dreadful personal experiences as Burakumin. The pieces appeared originally in the *Burakumin Liberation News*, a publication of a human rights organization based in Osaka. They are first-person narratives of confession and revelation, emotionally laden presentations of personal experience that reveal the pain and cruelty of name calling and raw prejudice.

The remaining short reading selections consist of four vignettes from *The House on Mango Street* by Sandra Cisneros. In these prose poems, a Latina adolescent confronts the poverty, alienation, identity crises, and family miseries that beset immigrant parents and their children as they experience the pain of poverty and gender discrimination at the same time.

When they are taken together, as they are in this instructional chapter, the stories of Richard Wright, Sue Sumii, Kenkichi Sakai, Susumu Yamamoto, and Sandra Cisneros testify to the universality of dehumanizing processes of discrimination. The lessons which accompany the chapter invite students to explore the power of words to reveal culture.

This chapter also encourages students to recognize, use, and share their own experiences by constructing their own autobiographies. By conceptualizing their personal experiences, using these experiences as subject matter, and, ultimately, sharing their experiences with others, students can cultivate communicative competence as well as discover a common humanity.

This chapter does not begin to exhaust the instructional potential of the reading selections, let alone that of the works from which they are excerpted. If these lessons do no more than encourage students to read the original works and derive more meaning from them, they will be a great success. On the most basic level, the reading selections may serve as composition models and testimonials to the capacity of these writers to transform traumatic and negative experiences into new literary forms and, through this process, help all of us envision new social possibilities.

Although we are fully aware of the dangers of overschematizing painful human experiences, we present the following chapter as a practical approach to prejudice and discrimination based on race, status, economic class, and gender. The eleven lessons in this chapter provide a series of opportunities for students to work together to confront prejudice. Because of the emotionally sensitive nature of the subject matter, we suggest that teachers create small work groups within the class setting for at least part of each lesson. Students working in collaborative groups will share their own experiences with prejudice more readily and feel less embarrassed about discussing the content of the reading selections than they will in open class discussions.

Because the narrative pull of each selection is so great, we have found that students often need time to digest the raw historical and personal data before such reflection can begin. We do not suggest that the teacher attempt to diminish the emotional impact of these selections. Because the narratives are so intense, students may use every opportunity to avoid their more upsetting messages and implications. With this in mind, we suggest that the teacher use a rather structured approach to direct the class's intellectual energies toward an analysis of content. The format suggested below has been useful.

> ***Define the content of the reading.*** *Identify the groups which constitute ingroups and outgroups in the reading. During the initial discussion of the reading, help students conceptualize the specific form prejudice takes in the narrative of oppression.*
>
> ***Identify techniques used to demean and insult.*** *What are the weapons the ingroup uses against the outgroup? How, if at all, has the outgroup internalized negative stereotypes?*
>
> ***Analyze the authors' craft.*** *What narrative techniques do they use to communicate the experience of prejudice? What codes do we as readers recognize and respond to? What perspectives do the authors reveal about the cultural values of the privileged ingroup and the victimized outgroup? How does the prose communicate the experience of discrimination? What do we as readers and as writers make of our growing awareness and sensitivity?*

The lessons in this chapter offer approaches to addressing these questions. We have designed them for use in secondary school classrooms across the curriculum—in language arts, social studies, multicultural or diversity courses, and foreign language classes.

Teachers may use the materials in the order we have suggested or select specific lessons or parts of lessons that meet their own instructional objectives. The lessons do not require consecutive conventional class periods. Also, some may be extended over several periods. Although these particular lessons focus on narratives of oppression created in Japan and the United States, there is no reason not to use others. A wealth of literature on prejudice and discrimination relative to other culture groups has been published in the United States and around the world. At several points we suggest related works that might enrich the course of study. We hope that teachers will add their own selections.

Conclusion

The experience of discrimination—whether as victim or victimizer—leaves residues of fury, sorrow, and shame that are painful to face. The study of narratives of oppression provides both the means to understand how prejudice and discrimination are sustained and reproduced and the means to overcome its more virulent forms. To come face-to-face with this dark side of human expression in the company of cultural others is to create educational circumstances that invite students to feel less isolated, to develop empathy and understanding for others, and to see themselves more clearly. As students study these narratives, they share the experience of discrimination, if only for a moment in time, with the writers and their subjects. By re-creating their own life stories in the language of autobiography and autobiographical fiction, they can learn to give voice to personal rage and grief and through this means understand and direct it. As teachers, we have a responsibility to raise such questions with our students and to help them search for better, more just, and dignifying social conditions than those that give rise to narratives of oppression in the first place.

Lesson 1—The Use of Name Calling and Pejorative Terms

Procedure

Divide the class into groups of three or four students each. Ask the groups to develop a definition of an epithet and provide two examples. This lesson usually elicits considerable silliness. Students will test the limits of classroom decorum as they struggle to determine what makes a word abusive.

Write on the chalkboard the list of epithets below, which includes at least one word from each of four areas of prejudice: status, race, class (poverty), and gender. Each student work group will define and discuss one word as a type of epithet and as a specific instrument used to identify a group of human beings. Inform the class that some of these words are related to the subject matter of the upcoming readings.

Assign one of the words to each work group. Designate the next ten minutes of class time for group work on the assigned word. Students will usually feel they know the meaning of these words. Encourage them to write down all the definitions of the word they can think of in one or two sentences. Then students should look up their assigned word in a good collegiate dictionary. In the case of phrases, what words seem to carry the disparaging content of the expression? The dictionary definition should suggest several different or additional definitions from the one(s) they have written out. After discussing the dictionary definitions, the group should think of at least two examples in which the assigned epithet might be used. At the end of the ten minutes, work groups should be prepared to report their findings to the class.

Questions for Discussion

1. Does the dictionary definition differ from the group's definition of the assigned epithet?
2. What circumstances in history or social setting might have caused this word to "go bad"?
3. What experiences, your own or those you have heard or read about, support the validity of either your original definition or the definition(s) you found in the dictionary?
    a. bastard
    b. nigger
    c. redneck
    d. indian giver
    e. to jew down
    f. bitch
    g. colored
    h. Uncle Tom

Exploring Further*

1. You may wish to assign this project to help students begin to see how words are used as weapons against oppressed groups. The overall aim of the assignment is to study the shifting nature of prejudice. Each student will choose a word for a brief assignment in etymology, directed toward consideration of the ways words "go bad." Encourage students to use a word that has changed to an insulting term in their social group or in society at large. Slang words such as *scum* and *bogus* and animal terms such as *birdbrain* and *pig* may be suggested. For students who cannot immediately think of a word to study, suggest some common terms such as *homely, nice, gossip, silly, gay,* and *fairy*—words whose meaning shift is clear in most dictionaries. Ask students to consider possible reasons for the shift in meaning.

* If students routinely keep a reading response or personal journal as part of their work for the class, these assignments will become part of that journal. If students do not keep such a journal, assignments may be required as homework.

Lesson 2–The Use of Language as an Instrument of Racial Prejudice

Reading Assignment

New: Readings 1–4 from Richard Wright's *Black Boy,* chapter 9 (see pages 66–77 for a full citation and the readings)

Procedure

The lesson begins with a discussion of the literal and connotative meanings of the words in the title, *Black Boy.* Students will discuss the meanings of *black* and *boy.* Students who work frequently in collaborative groups will find this an interesting exercise to complete with peers they know and trust. (See questions 1–3.)

Students will read silently the four selections from *Black Boy,* making a list of demeaning words as they read. Most students will include on their list the words *nigger, bastard, sonofabitch.* Students should also note but not necessarily discuss *thing, prick, hell, Yankee, white, black, Negro.* (See questions 4–7.)

Questions for Discussion

1. Do you think Richard Wright used these words in 1945 in the same sense we understand them today? Why or why not?
2. Think back on your own experience. In what ways have the meanings of the words *black* and *boy* changed as you have grown older and broadened your experience?
3. Considering the shifts in the meanings of words, do you think these words will continue to change in meaning? Why or why not?
4. Ask the students to compile a class list which includes all the demeaning terms they have discovered in the reading.
5. Ask students to form groups and assign each group two words from the class list to define, analyze, and discuss. If a set of college-edition dictionaries is available, ask students to explore the etymology of some of the words, one or two terms per group. Ask them to look for the following information:
    a. Are there words with roots that suggest these words were not initially instruments of prejudice?
    b. Have either of the words changed in meaning over time?
    c. Do the words have more than one meaning?
6. Ask each group to report what they have learned to the class.
7. Ask the class to consider to what degree the circumstance in which they use a word matters. For example, ask them to consider the word *thing* from page 74.

Exploring Further

1. Students will complete a short investigation into name-calling. Students will respond in a one-page journal entry to the rhyme,

    Sticks and stones may break my bones,
    but names can never hurt me.

2. Ask students over the next week to document the evidence of prejudice as it appears in their own communities. Students should record at least two examples of pejorative labeling as they discover it in written form and two examples of name-calling as they overhear it in their social environment. An investigation and exploration of visual graffiti in this framework is especially interesting in art classes or as part of an interdisciplinary study.

Lesson 3—The Use of Language as an Instrument of Prejudice against an Oppressed Minority Group in a Different Cultural Setting

Reading Assignment

New: Readings 5–7 from Sue Sumii's *The River with No Bridge* (see pages 78–92 for a full citation and the readings); Student Handout: The Burakumin of Japan (see pages 100–102)

Review: Readings 1–3, Wright

Questions for Discussion

1. What is a *ghetto*?
2. What specific characteristics of a *ghetto* does the village of Komori manifest?
3. To what in your experience can you relate the status of *eta*?
4. What groups of people in history were forced to live in specific parts of a city or areas of the countryside?
5. What is the basis for low-status minority group prejudice? Discuss as many examples as you can remember from your readings in history and in current events.
6. Compare the prejudice you identified in the Richard Wright readings to that of the Sumii readings.
7. Few Americans can hear the word *nigger* without a violent reaction. In Japan the word *eta* produces the same level of pain and outrage. Discuss words as emotional triggers and ways in which these terms may take on added meaning when they cross cultures. Compare terms like *nazi, indian giver,* and *gypsy.*
8. In cultural settings cleanliness often becomes symbolic. Richard is considered a "dirty nigger." Koji and his friends are accused of being dirty, of stinking, yet one of the readings revolves around the family bath. Where do we get our ideas about what is "clean" and what is "dirty"? Why are these young men considered "dirty"? Do they see themselves as "dirty"?

Exploring Further

1. Assign two one-page journal entries, analyzing (1) Griggs' rhyme,

   All these white folks dressed so fine
   Their ass-holes smell just like mine (Wright, 71).

and (2) Hirokichi's meditative,

> *Funny what a difference there is between people when we're all the same human beings. There they are, treating the Emperor's crap like treasure, but in our case, they think even the rice we grow is dirty and stinks* (Sumii, 86).

2. Divide the class into groups, assign each group one of Sumii's or Wright's readings (seven readings in all), and ask each group to search in their reading for instances of language as an instrument of prejudice in one of the cultural settings. Groups will then report to the class on their findings and compare the use of racial epithets in Japan and the United States. Remind students that this analysis is not a contest to see which setting is better or worse in name calling.

Lesson 4—The Use of Language as an Instrument of Prejudice by Singling Out One Characteristic or Feature of Appearance

Reading Assignment

New: Reading 8 from Kenkichi Sakai, "Having Excrement Thrown over Me" (see page 93 for a full citation and the reading)

Review: Reading 4, Wright; Readings 5–7, Sumii

Questions for Discussion

Wright: Reading 4

1. What stereotype is Reynolds alluding to regarding the length of Richard's penis?
2. Richard is aware he is being reduced to an animal. He says, "I had heard the whites regarded Negroes as animals in sex matters and his words made me angry." Why is he angry?
3. What are the implications of the bull/cow imagery?
4. Reynolds suggests Richard can spin "like a top." How does this sequence of comparisons of a body part from animal to toy work to further demean Richard?

Sumii: Readings 5–7

5. Why does the damage to Yaé, Nanaé's doll, cause such hysterics?
6. Why is being called a name like "Four Fingers" such an insult?
7. Which members of the family are most aware of the meaning of the damage and the cause of the hysterics? Defend your answer.
8. How is excrement used to universalize the human condition in Sumii's Reading 6?

Sakai: Reading 8

9. How is excrement used to degrade, literally and figuratively, in the selection by Sakai? Who is doing the degrading? Who is being degraded?
10. Why does Sakai think he is different when he is told, "Touch your ass. There's a tail there"?

General Questions

11. How does each author use the subject of excrement to make a different point?
12. Why do you think despised groups are often identified with body parts? What body parts are used in this way in Wright? in Sumii? in Sakai?
13. Is animal imagery a basis for insult in contemporary culture? What animal comparison would you find personally insulting?

14. As we have seen in our reading, one way to dehumanize is to reduce human beings to a single characteristic or feature of appearance, origin, or gender, to identify the person by something that is only a part rather than the totality. How do "bad words" illustrate this truth? Relate your answer to our readings in this unit.

Exploring Further

1. Ask students to make a list of idioms or expressions employing animal images that they have heard at school or elsewhere. The list must include at least two compliments such as "brave as a lion" and two insults such as "mousy brown hair." Although there will be considerable duplication of expressions, students will also find many new ones. Ask the students to share their lists with the class. This assignment can develop into a poem or other creative writing exercise.

Lesson 5—Autobiography as Used to Portray Racial Prejudice and Discrimination

Reading Assignment

Review: Readings 1–4, Wright

Questions for Discussion

Wright: Reading 1

1. Why does Richard take this job?
2. What happens to the black woman?
3. What is the significance of the lack of reaction of passing white people and the policeman?
4. What is Richard thinking as he stares at the bloody floor?
5. Why does the boss's son offer Richard a cigarette and light it?

Wright: Reading 2

6. What do you think would have happened if Richard had said, "Oh, no, sir," when asked if he wanted a drink?
7. What is the significance of *sir* in this reading?
8. To what extent is alcohol a catalyst to the men's behavior?
9. Why does the policeman stop Richard on his bicycle?
10. What does the boss's son mean when he says, "I don't like your looks"?

Wright: Reading 3

11. How does Griggs survive and keep his job?
12. What is Griggs' advice for Richard?
13. Why does Richard resist Griggs' advice?
14. Griggs says he is not an "Uncle Tom." What does he mean and how does he justify his claim?
15. Griggs sings a song. What does the song mean?

Wright: Reading 4

16. According to Griggs, what are Richard's qualifications for the job at the optical company?
17. What does Richard mean by "Maybe that's what's wrong with Negroes. They take too much time"?
18. Why is it important that Richard is working for a Yankee?
19. What does Richard hope for in this new job?
20. What is Richard's greatest "sin" with regard to white people? Again, Richard's alleged omission of *Mr.* when addressing Pease and the men's threats result in Richard quitting the job. What is the significance of the titles of address in the white world of the early twentieth-century South?

Exploring Further

1. Assign or direct students to find an article about race prejudice in a current newspaper story or magazine article. If students do not have ready access to newspaper sources, duplicate a story that lends itself to the same kind of close reading analysis the class has undertaken with the reading selections in this lesson. Encourage students to read the article carefully, being especially alert for examples of language that reflect prejudice. Students should summarize the article in their journals (or on a separate piece of paper) and provide a full source citation so they can find the article again or, better yet, cut out the article and attach it to their paper. After reading, summarizing, and citing their article, students should relate the subject matter of this article to the experiences recounted by Richard Wright and, if appropriate, to their personal experiences.
2. Assign or direct students to find a poem or short story about race prejudice. Students should read the work carefully, being especially alert for examples of language that reflects prejudice. Students then paraphrase the poem or summarize the short story. Finally, they will relate the subject matter of the selected work to the experiences recounted by Richard Wright and, if appropriate, to their personal experiences.

Lesson 6—Autobiography as Used to Portray Discrimination against an Oppressed Minority Group Not Based on Race

Reading Assignment

Review: Readings 5–7, Sumii; Reading 8, Sakai

Questions for Discussion

Sumii: Reading 5

1. What starts the conflict in the schoolyard?
2. Who instigates the conflict in the schoolyard?
3. Who is blamed for the conflict?
4. Why do Seitaro and Toyota not immediately explain their reasons for fighting?
5. What do the words *stink* and *stinking* imply in Reading 5? In what contexts do they occur and why? What is the significance of the words?

Sumii: Reading 6

6. What is the significance of Hirokichi's story about the emperor?
7. In Reading 5 the children laugh about the ox dung, jeering, "Of course an ox drops ox dung." How is this response different from that of the people at Fudé's in the emperor story in Reading 6?
8. What distinction concerning fatherless children does Hirokichi clarify for Koji?
9. In what sense is it better to be a *bastard* than to live in Komori?
10. What do the words *stink* and *stinking* imply in Reading 2? In what contexts do they occur and why?

Sumii: Reading 7

11. When the children visit their grandfather Soshichi in the neighboring village of Ino, what most impresses Koji about the house?
12. Is it true that the grandfather is an *eta*? Comment on the following: "I wonder if they're all *eta* at Grandad's. Master Hidé, the priest's son, said all the relatives of Komori people are *eta* too, but they look well-off here."
13. What future does the grandfather see for Koji?
14. What future does Koji see for himself?
15. Why is Nanaé devastated that her doll has lost its thumb?

Sakai: Reading 8

16. Children learn about prejudice as they grow up. At what age is Sakai aware of discrimination against his *Buraku* (village)? At what age does he run away from his village to the big city of Osaka? Do these ages seem typical for what he must undertake to deal with the prejudice he comes to recognize?
17. The servants ask him, "Do you know where you come from?" Why is this a "final blow"?
18. What do the servants imply when they say, "Even if we kill you, we won't be guilty of any crime"?
19. Comment on the passage in paragraph 3: "Since I am one of those human beings called 'Eta' whom people discriminate against, whatever they do to me, I am not even 'qualified' to complain."
20. Why is it easy for an oppressed group to believe what their aggressors say about them, for example, "So I got it into my head that we were after all a different kind of human being"?
21. Can you think of other oppressed groups where discrimination is based not on race but on some other criteria, such as geography?

Exploring Further

1. Articles about discrimination against a minority group not based on race, gender, or class may be difficult to find. Therefore, you may want to assign an article or story that lends itself to the same kind of close reading analysis the class has undertaken with the reading selections in this lesson. Encourage students to read the article or story carefully, being especially alert for examples of language that reflect prejudice. Students should summarize the article in their journals and provide a full source citation so they can find the article again, then try to relate the subject matter of this article to the experiences recounted by Sue Sumii and, if appropriate, to their personal experiences.

Lesson 7–Autobiography as Used to Portray Gender Discrimination

Reading Assignment

New: Readings 10 and 12 from Sandra Cisneros's *The House on Mango Street,* "My Name" and "Beautiful and Cruel" (see pages 95–96 and 98 for a full citation and the readings)

Questions for Discussion

Cisneros: Reading 10

1. In what specific way, according to Esperanza, are the Chinese and Mexicans alike?
2. Esperanza compares her great-grandmother to a "wild horse" and a "fancy chandelier." What do these comparisons mean?
3. What does Esperanza see as proof that her great-grandmother was "a wild horse of a woman"? To what extent could her great-grandmother express resistance to marriage?
4. Why does Cisneros use the expression "sit their sadness on an elbow"? What makes this metaphor so powerful?
5. Esperanza has inherited her great-grandmother's name. What does she not want to inherit and why? Tie your answer (if possible) to the metaphor in question 3.

Cisneros: Reading 12

6. In what ways are Esperanza (the speaker) and her sister Nenny different?
7. What desire do the sisters share? Why is it easier for Nenny "to talk that way"?
8. What hope for the future does her mother offer Esperanza?
9. What power does the "one with red lips" possess?
10. What war has Esperanza started? Why is it quiet? Why do you think Cisneros chose the metaphor she used in the last sentence?

Exploring Further

1. Ask students to write their own vignette beginning with the last sentence of "Beautiful and Cruel": "I am one who leaves the table like a man, without putting back the chair or picking up the plate."
2. Ask students to write one page about why Cisneros juxtaposes *beauty* and *cruelty*.

Lesson 8—Autobiography as Used to Portray Economic Class Discrimination

Reading Assignment

New: Reading 9 from Susumi Yamamoto, "My Experiences of Discrimination" (see page 94 for a full citation and the reading); Reading 11 from Cisneros's *The House on Mango Street,* "Bums in the Attic" (see page 97 for the reading)

Review: Readings 5–7, Sumii

Questions for Discussion

Sumii: Reading 5

1. The older children in the schoolyard fight recognize the economic disparity between the children from Komori and the other children. How is that disparity emphasized in the preparations the families made for quartering the soldiers on maneuvers?
2. How is food discussed in this regard in a manner meant to alienate the children from Komori?

Sumii: Reading 6

3. What evidence do we have of poverty in Seitaro's and Koji's household in Komori? Students will want to discuss the practice of communal bathing, a practice not limited to the Burakumin. A bath is a luxury allowed only twice a month. Why is a bath such an expensive undertaking in Komori? Students should also be reminded to note Fude's assumption that everyone will bathe before she finally takes her turn.

Sumii: Reading 7

4. The visiting children are acutely aware of the better economic circumstances of their grandparents. What makes the house and its surroundings seem more luxurious than their own? What foods are they given that are seen as especially luxurious? What is the source of Koji's confusion about his grandparents' comparative wealth?

Yamamoto: Reading 9

5. Yamamoto does not place the entire blame for his suffering on discrimination. What historical and personal events complicate and intensify the discrimination he endures?
6. As an elementary school student, what two items does he mention having to do without? Would the lack of these items keep you from going to school? Why or why not?
7. When Yamamoto cannot pay for his school trip, what does the teacher suggest and why does Yamamoto resist the teacher's suggestion?

8. Yamamoto's poverty causes him to suffer severe physical problems. What are these problems? What other physical problems arise from the kind of poverty associated with economic discrimination?

Cisneros: Reading 11

9. Esperanza describes her family as "staring out the window like the hungry." What do you think she means by this statement?
10. When Mama begins "When we win the lottery," the speaker "stops listening." What does the lottery signify to many of the nation's poor? Why?
11. The "people who live on hills so close to the stars," according to Esperanza, "forget those of us who live too much on earth." What specific things can the people who live on hills "forget"?
12. Notice that Esperanza, like Yamamoto, feels shame over her poverty. What sort of a future does the speaker plan for herself?

Exploring Further

1. Ask the students to think of someone they know who suffers discrimination from being poor. Ask them to try to put themselves in that person's shoes and imagine "walking in those shoes" for an entire day, then describe that day in first-person narrative form.

Lesson 9—Autobiography as Used to Portray Discrimination through Violence

Reading Assignment

Review: Readings 1, 2, and 4, Wright; Reading 5, Sumii; Reading 8, Sakai; Reading 10, Cisneros

Questions for Discussion

Wright: Readings 1, 2, and 4

1. In Reading 1 a woman is beaten, perhaps raped. To what extent is the physical violence against her an example of gender, race, or ethnic discrimination/hatred? The boss "slapped" Richard "reassuringly on the back." What do you perceive to be the motive for this "friendly" gesture?
2. In Reading 2 Richard does not foresee the violence against him. Why not? What excuse does the white man give Richard for beating him? In the second and third "scenes" in this reading, when Richard is challenged by white men, he is very careful to use the "magic word." What is the word and does it stem the violence against him? Language can both cause and divert violence. How does the language used by the white men in this reading enflame violence?
3. In Reading 4 an older Richard is verbally and physically abused by two white coworkers. Ostensibly, his crime is still in his language. Explain the language trap set for him by Pease and Reynolds. Do you agree with Richard that the accusation against him is only pretense and the real aim is to force him to quit the job?

Sumii: Reading 5

4. Who do you think starts the fight? Do you think Toyota and Seitaro are justified in fighting? Is there ever justification in using violence? What would you have done in the boys' place?

Sakai: Reading 8

5. In "Having Excrement Thrown over Me," physical violence takes the specific form of defilement. Sakai is also beaten and verbally abused. Which form of abuse do you think would be more difficult to bear, the verbal or the physical abuse?

Cisneros: Reading 10

6. In "My Name," Esperanza describes the physical violence inflicted on her great-grandmother. Is this physical violence different from that suffered by Richard? by Sakai? by Toyota and Seitaro? Identify ways in which oppressed minorities are vulnerable to physical violence. Are children (Richard on his bicycle and the Burakumin children on the playground) and women (Esperanza's great-grandmother) more likely to suffer physical violence than men?

General Question

7. Physical violence is often inflicted with the claim, either implied or stated, that the violence "is for your own good" or will "be a lesson to you"—that the perpetrator has the best interests of the victim at heart. Consider each of the readings. Can you detect such a claim in any of these readings?

Exploring Further

1. Students will write two narratives in their journals. First, recount an instance of discrimination, either personally experienced or observed, consisting of verbal violence ("fightin' words"). In this narrative the violence must be limited to taunts and does not include physical attack. Then, recount an instance of discrimination, either personally experienced or observed, involving defilement or another form of violent physical attack. In each narrative be sure to examine the source of the violence, the object of the violence, and the result of the violence. Could this violent episode have been avoided? Encourage students to be as specific in their reflections on the conflict as possible.

Lesson 10—Reactions to Prejudice and Discrimination

Reading Assignment

New: Reading 13 from Sandra Cisneros's *The House on Mango Street,* "Mango Says Goodbye Sometimes" (see page 99 for the reading)

Review: Readings 3–4, Wright; Readings 5–6, Sumii; Reading 8, Sakai; Reading 9, Yamamoto

Procedure

This lesson looks at the autobiographical materials in the chapter from a slightly different point of view. It assumes that the readings have already been explored in depth as a basis for the study of prejudice and discrimination. The characters in these readings appear to have several reactions to being the objects of discrimination. In this lesson students are asked to consider the way the narrators and other characters respond.

Begin the lesson by asking students to reread the selected passages. Using the chalkboard or flipchart, write up three types or categories of responses to discrimination. Type 1 includes shame, hopelessness, frustration, surrender. Type 2 suggests more active responses such as anger, passive resistance, and active fighting back. Type 3 includes possibilities such as dignity, an ability to rise above oppression, and the determination to change the situation.

Working in small groups, the students will discuss the following questions and try to categorize the characters' responses into the categories above. Students may want to share in their groups their own reactions to discrimination. As the class returns to a general group discussion, consider the possibility of a developmental progression from the first type of response through the second and finally to the third.

Questions for Discussion

Wright: Readings 3–4

1. When Griggs admonishes Richard to learn how to live in the South, to "get out of white people's way," how does Richard react to his advice? What category from the typology is most representative of Griggs' reaction to discrimination?
2. Discuss Richard's conversation with Mr. Crane after he has been forced to quit his job in the optical company. Why does Richard feel "drenched in shame, naked to my soul. The whole of my being...violated..."?
3. Why do you think Mr. Crane chooses to work in the South? Why do you think Griggs stays in the South? Does this have anything to do with how he reacts to discrimination? What does Richard's resolve to move to the North tell us about him? Support your answers from the text as well as from your own experiences.

4. In all of the readings from *Black Boy,* Richard does his best to survive with dignity and escapes his oppressors, despite the treatment he receives. Writers often use vision and the ability to see symbolically. In what symbolic ways does the narrator "see"? In what ways are Mr. Crane, Pease, and Reynolds "blind"?

Sumii: Readings 5–6

5. Why do Toyota and Seitaro eventually defend their actions to Mr. Egawa, the teacher? Why do they wait so long and endure so much before they do speak up? What is the result of their efforts?
6. In Reading 6 from *The River with No Bridge* the village adults support each other by sharing baths and tea and stories. How does the presence of a supportive community mediate the effects of oppression? What effect does humor have in this situation?

Sakai: Reading 8

7. Sakai writes, "Since I am one of those human beings called 'Eta' whom people discriminate against, whatever they do to me, I am not even 'qualified' to complain." How would you categorize this response? His mother advises him, "Wherever you go, you're in an impossible situation (i.e., you can't escape discrimination). Stay here and just do as I say." How does Sakai's response to discrimination differ from that of his mother? Does he follow his mother's advice? At the time of the writing, how old is the narrator? What does Sakai's attitude toward his mother reveal about his response to discrimination?

Yamamoto: Reading 9

8. What effect did discovery of the liberation movement have on Yamamoto's outlook?

Cisneros: Reading 13

9. As the narrator determines to break free of the poverty that has held her down, what will her escape route be? Why and how will she return to help "the ones I left behind. For the ones who cannot out"?

Exploring Further

1. Ask students to write a one-page narrative about someone's reaction to prejudice and/or discrimination. Students can write about themselves, someone they know, a character in one of the readings, or a famous person. The narrative should include a critique of the reaction as well as description.

Lesson 11–Writing

Part 1

Writing an autobiographical essay in which the narrator recognizes and conceptualizes prejudice

Procedure

Students working in writing groups or teams will share experiences appropriate for autobiographical writing. These may come from personal experience, observation, or family stories. During this brainstorming session each student will compile a personal list of at least five relevant experiences. Students need to review ways of shaping and distancing their personal experiences, as their narratives will be shared with the teacher and the class.

As students begin to develop their lists of ideas, encourage them to be risk takers and supportive peers. At the same time, the class should consider legal issues of privacy and good taste. Teachers should be especially sensitive to restrictions on disclosure of personal information and to teacher responsibility concerning criminal acts, especially child abuse. Students are likely to be more at ease and open if the groups have been working together on other assignments. However, the teacher will need to monitor group interaction carefully.

Questions for Students to Consider in Conceptualizing and Writing the Autobiographical Essay

1. Point of view—Who is telling this story? Consider the status, race, gender, and age of the narrator. Is the narrator the author? Another character in the story? An outside observer? Omniscient? Why does it matter?
2. Setting: time—When is this story taking place? Consider the issues that change as we grow older or look back on an experience that happened in the past.
3. Setting: place—Where is this story taking place? Are we being shown a ghetto? Are we being shown a family, a school, or a workplace?
4. Plot development—How much time is being covered in this story?

Homework Assignment

Each student will draft a three- to five-page autobiographical narrative recounting a personal experience with discrimination if possible, or an observed experience or experience recounted to them by someone else if necessary. Students are encouraged to consider one of their narratives from earlier homework assignments which they feel, with revision and polishing, would be appropriate for peer evaluation and discussion at the next class session. Students should also be encouraged to review their class notes for potential topics.

Part 2

Editing the autobiographical essay based on an experience of prejudice

Procedure

Students will continue to work in their writing groups, sharing their draft narratives. Members of the group are expected to offer each other suggestions for revision and improvement.

Questions on Technique for Students to Consider in the Group Revision Process

1. Is the author using language and the autobiographical narrative to demonstrate prejudice or discrimination due to gender, oppressed minority group status, race, or economic class?
2. Is the author using language and/or acts such as physical violence, pejorative labeling, reduction to body parts or animal status, or a particular characteristic or feature of appearance to tell the story?
3. Is the author describing prejudice through demeaning accounts of a specific culture or national or ethnic group?
4. Is there an undercurrent of the symbolism of survival and dignity or of hopelessness and defeat in the narrative?

Homework Assignment

Using suggestions for revisions from the writing group and the teacher, each student will complete a final draft of the personal narrative.

Part 3

Sharing the autobiographical essay about prejudice

Procedure

Students will share their personal narratives. Before any essays are shared, students need to discuss the value of sharing painful encounters as they learn to overcome prejudice and experience the healing that knowledge and education in the best sense allow them to achieve together. Individual students must not be forced to read their essays to the group. However, encouragement from the writing group and the teacher will often convince even reluctant students to share their essays. Students who do must receive positive and supportive feedback.

All students should have ample opportunity to share their essays, perhaps over several class periods, as shy students may need time to rally their courage. As a closure activity, students may respond to the questions for discussion below. These questions can be assigned for homework or for small-group work.

Questions for Discussion

1. Would you share this essay with your family? Why or why not?
2. Would you share this essay with other students? With other classes? Why or why not?
3. To what extent does the age of your listening public matter to you?
4. Will you "publish" this essay? Why?

Selected Readings for Cultural Understanding

Richard Wright: Readings from *Black Boy*

Chapter 9 from *Black Boy (American Hunger): A Record of Childhood and Youth* by Richard Wright. New York: Harper & Brothers, 1945. Restored text established by the Library of America for the Harper Perennial edition, 1993.

Introduction

Richard Wright (1908-1960) was already an important writer deeply involved in the literary and political life of the United States when he completed the autobiographical work entitled *American Hunger* in December 1943. When the Book-of-the-Month-Club told Wright's publisher it would accept only the first section describing Wright's experiences of growing up in the South, Wright changed the title to *Black Boy*. The second section, telling of Wright's life in Chicago, was published as *American Hunger* by Harper & Row in 1977. When the translation of *Black Boy* by Gallimard won the French Critics' Award, Wright was already living abroad. When Wright died in 1960, a copy of *Black Boy* was cremated along with his body and interred with his ashes. Wright's work was published in its entirety for the first time in October 1991 by the Library of America.

Efforts by historians and literary critics to establish the historical "truth" of Richard Wright's autobiographical novel, *Black Boy,* continue. To study the work we need not, indeed cannot, determine the extent to which Wright consciously or unconsciously shaped the story of his life to create a representative myth of an intelligent, sensitive, and tortured black male growing up in an historical period and geographical location pervaded by racism. We do have basic biographical data and we can appreciate his artistry.

We have selected chapter 9 for inclusion. The order of the text has not been altered nor has the text been abridged.

Reading 1

Chapter 9 (pages 212–13)

My life now depended upon my finding work, and I was so anxious that I accepted the first offer, a job as a porter in a clothing store selling cheap goods to Negroes on credit. The shop was always crowded with black men and women pawing over cheap suits and dresses. And they paid whatever price the white man asked. The boss, his son, and the clerk treated the Negroes with open contempt, pushing, kicking, or slapping them. No matter how often I witnessed it, I could not get used to it. How can they accept it? I asked myself. I kept on edge, trying to stifle my feelings and never quite succeeding, a prey to guilt and fear because I felt that the boss suspected that I resented what I saw.

One morning, while I was polishing brass out front, the boss and his son drove up in their car. A frightened black woman sat between them. They got out and half dragged and half kicked the woman into the store. White people passed and looked on without expression. A white policeman watched from the corner, twirling his night stick; but he made no move. I watched out of the corner of my eyes, but I never slackened the strokes of my chamois upon the brass. After a moment or two I heard shrill screams coming from the rear room of the store; later the woman stumbled out, bleeding, crying, holding her stomach, her clothing torn. When she reached the sidewalk, the policeman met her, grabbed her, accused her of being drunk, called a patrol wagon and carted her away.

When I went to the rear of the store, the boss and his son were washing their hands at the sink. They looked at me and laughed uneasily. The floor was bloody, strewn with wisps of hair and clothing. My face must have reflected my shock, for the boss slapped me reassuringly on the back.

"Boy, that's what we do to niggers when they don't pay their bills," he said.

His son looked at me and grinned.

"Here, hava cigarette," he said.

Not knowing what to do, I took it. He lit his and held the match for me. This was a gesture of kindness, indicating that, even if they had beaten the black woman, they would not beat me if I knew enough to keep my mouth shut.

"Yes, sir," I said.

After they had gone, I sat on the edge of a packing box and stared at the bloody floor until the cigarette went out.

Reading 2

Chapter 9 (pages 213–16)

The store owned a bicycle which I used in delivering purchases. One day, while returning from the suburbs, my bicycle tire was punctured. I walked along the hot, dusty road, sweating and leading the bicycle by the handle bars.

A car slowed at my side.

"What's the matter there, boy?" a white man called.

I told him that my bicycle was broken and that I was walking back to town.

"That's too bad," he said. "Hop on the running board."

He stopped the car. I clutched hard at my bicycle with one hand and clung to the side of the car with the other.

"All set?"

"Yes, sir."

The car started. It was full of young white men. They were drinking. I watched the flask pass from mouth to mouth.

"Wanna drink, boy?" one asked.

The memory of my six-year-old drinking came back and filled me with caution. But I laughed, the wind whipping my face.

"Oh, no!" I said.

The words were barely out of my mouth before I felt something hard and cold smash me between the eyes. It was an empty whisky bottle. I saw stars, and fell backwards from the speeding car into the dust of the road, my feet becoming entangled in the steel spokes of the bicycle. The car stopped and the white men piled out and stood over me.

"Nigger, ain't you learned no better sense'n that yet?" asked the man who hit me. "Ain't you learned to say *sir* to a white man yet?"

Dazed, I pulled to my feet. My elbows and legs were bleeding. Fists doubled, the white man advanced, kicking the bicycle out of the way.

"Aw, leave the bastard alone. He's got enough," said one.

They stood looking at me. I rubbed my shins, trying to stop the flow of blood. No doubt they felt a sort of contemptuous pity, for one asked:

"You wanna ride to town now, nigger? You reckon you know enough to ride now?"

"I wanna walk," I said simply.

Maybe I sounded funny. They laughed.

"Well, walk, you black sonofabitch!"

Before they got back into their car, they comforted me with:

"Nigger, you sure ought to be glad it was us you talked to that way. You're a lucky bastard, 'cause if you'd said that to some other white man, you might've been a dead nigger now."

I was learning rapidly how to watch white people, to observe their every move, every fleeting expression, how to interpret what was said and what left unsaid.

* * * * *

Late one Saturday night I made some deliveries in a white neighborhood. I was pedaling my bicycle back to the store as fast as I could when a police car, swerving toward me, jammed me into the curbing.

"Get down, nigger, and put up your hands!" they ordered.

I did. They climbed out of the car, guns drawn, faces set, and advanced slowly.

"Keep still!" they ordered.

I reached my hands higher. They searched my pockets and packages. They seemed dissatisfied when they could find nothing incriminating. Finally, one of them said:

"Boy, tell your boss not to send you out in white neighborhoods at this time of night."

"Yes, sir," I said.

I rode off, feeling that they might shoot at me, feeling that the pavement might disappear. It was like living in a dream, the reality of which might change at any moment.

* * * * *

Each day in the store I watched the brutality with growing hate, yet trying to keep my feelings from registering in my face. When the boss looked at me I would avoid his eyes. Finally the boss's son cornered me one morning.

"Say, nigger, look here," he began.

"Yes, sir."

"What's on your mind?"

"Nothing, sir," I said, trying to look amazed, trying to fool him.

"Why don't you laugh and talk like the other niggers?" he asked.

"Well, sir, there's nothing much to say or smile about," I said, smiling.

His face was hard, baffled; I knew that I had not convinced him. He whirled from me and went to the front of the store; he came back a moment later, his face red. He tossed a few green bills at me.

"I don't like your looks, nigger. Now, get!" he snapped.

I picked up the money and did not count it. I grabbed my hat and left.

Reading 3

Chapter 9 (pages 216–19)

I held a series of petty jobs for short periods, quitting some to work elsewhere, being driven off others because of my attitude, my speech, the look in my eyes. I was no nearer than ever to my goal of saving enough money to leave. At times I doubted if I could ever do it.

One jobless morning I went to my old classmate, Griggs, who worked for a Capitol Street jeweler. He was washing the windows of the store when I came upon him.

"Do you know where I can find a job?" I asked.

He looked at me with scorn.

"Yes, I know where you can find a job," he said, laughing.

"Where?"

"But I wonder if you can hold it," he said.

"What do you mean?" I asked. "Where's the job?"

"Take your time," he said. "You know, Dick, I know you. You've been trying to hold a job all summer, and you can't. Why? Because you're impatient. That's your big fault."

I said nothing, because he was repeating what I had already heard him say. He lit a cigarette and blew out smoke leisurely.

"Well," I said, egging him on to speak.

"I wish to hell I could talk to you," he said.

"I think I know what you want to tell me," I said.

He clapped me on the shoulder; his face was full of fear, hate, concern for me.

"Do you want to get killed?" he asked me.

"Hell, no!"

"Then, for God's sake, learn how to live in the South!"

"What do you mean?" I demanded. "Let white people tell me that. Why should you?"

"See?" he said triumphantly, pointing his finger at me. "There it is, *now!* It's in your face. You won't let people tell you things. You rush too much. I'm trying to help you and you won't let me." He paused and looked about; the streets were filled with white people. He spoke to me in a low, full tone. "Dick, look, you're black, black, *black*, see? Can't you understand that?"

"Sure. I understand it," I said.

"You don't act a damn bit like it," he spat.

He then reeled off an account of my actions on every job I had held that summer.

"How did you know that?" I asked.

"White people make it their business to watch niggers," he explained. "And they pass the word around. Now, my boss is a Yankee and he tells me things. You're marked already."

Could I believe him? Was it true? How could I ever learn this strange world of white people?

"Then tell me how must I act?" I asked humbly. "I just want to make enough money to leave."

"Wait and I'll tell you," he said.

At that moment a woman and two men stepped from the jewelry store; I moved to one side to let them pass, my mind intent upon Griggs's words. Suddenly Griggs reached for my arm and jerked me violently, sending me stumbling three or four feet across the pavement. I whirled.

"What's the matter with you?" I asked.

Griggs glared at me, then laughed.

"I'm teaching you how to get out of white people's way," he said.

I looked at the people who had come out of the store; yes, they were *white,* but I had not noticed it.

"Do you see what I mean?" he asked. "White people want you out of their way." He pronounced the words slowly so that they would sink into my mind.

"I know what you mean," I breathed.

"Dick, I'm treating you like a brother," he said. "You act around white people as if you didn't know that they were white. And they *see* it."

"Oh, Christ, I can't be a slave," I said hopelessly.

"But you've got to eat," he said.

"Yes, I got to eat."

"Then start acting like it," he hammered at me, pounding his fist in his palm. "When you're in front of white people, *think* before you act, *think* before you speak. Your way of doing things is all right among *our* people, but not for *white* people. They won't stand for it."

I stared bleakly into the morning sun. I was nearing my seventeenth birthday and I was wondering if I would ever be free of this plague. What Griggs was saying was true, but it was simply utterly impossible for me to calculate, to scheme, to act, to plot all the time. I would remember to dissemble for short periods, then I would forget and act straight and human again, not with the desire to harm anybody, but merely forgetting the artificial status of race and class. It was the same with whites as with blacks; it was my way with everybody. I sighed, looking at the glittering diamonds in the store window, the rings and the neat rows of golden watches.

"I guess you're right," I said at last. "I've got to watch myself, break myself...."

"No," he said quickly, feeling guilty now. Someone—a white man—went into the store and we paused in our talk. "You know, Dick, you may think I'm an Uncle Tom, but I'm not. I hate these white people, hate 'em with all my heart. But I can't show it; if I did, they'd kill me." He paused and looked around to see if there were any white people within hearing distance. "Once I heard an old drunk nigger say:

All these white folks dressed so fine
Their ass-holes smell just like mine....

Reading 4

Chapter 9 (pages 219–28)

I laughed uneasily, looking at the white faces that passed me. But Griggs, when he laughed, covered his mouth with his hand and bent at the knees, a gesture which was unconsciously meant to conceal his excessive joy in the presence of whites.

"That's how I feel about 'em," he said proudly after he had finished his spasm of glee. He grew sober. "There's an optical company upstairs and the boss is a Yankee from Illinois. Now, he wants a boy to work all day in summer, mornings and evenings in winter. He wants to break a colored boy into the optical trade. You know algebra and you're just cut out for the work. I'll tell Mr. Crane about you and I'll get in touch with you."

"Do you suppose I could see him now?" I asked.

"For God's sake, take your *time!*" he thundered at me.

"Maybe that's what's wrong with Negroes," I said. "They take too much time."

I laughed, but he was disturbed. I thanked him and left. For a week I did not hear from him and I gave up hope. Then one afternoon Griggs came to my house.

"It looks like you've got a job," he said. "You're going to have a chance to learn a trade. But remember to keep your head. Remember you're black. You start tomorrow."

"What will I get?"

"Five dollars a week to start with; they'll raise you if they like you," he explained.

My hopes soared. Things were not quite so bad, after all. I would have a chance to learn a trade. And I need not give up school. I told him that I would take the job, that I would be humble.

"You'll be working for a Yankee and you ought to get along," he said.

The next morning I was outside the office of the optical company long before it opened. I was reminding myself that I must be polite, must think before I spoke, must think before I acted, must say "yes sir, no sir," that I must so conduct myself that white people would not think that I thought I was as good as they. Suddenly a white man came up to me.

"What do you want?" he asked me.

"I'm reporting for a job, sir," I said.

"O.K. Come on."

I followed him up a flight of steps and he unlocked the door of the office. I was a little tense, but the young white man's manner put me at ease and I sat and held my hat in my hand. A white girl came and began punching the typewriter. Soon another white man, thin and gray, entered and went into the rear room. Finally a tall, red-faced white man arrived, shot me a quick glance and sat at his desk. His brisk manner branded him a Yankee.

"You're the new boy, eh?"

"Yes, sir."

"Let me get my mail out of the way and I'll talk with you," he said pleasantly.

"Yes, sir."

I even pitched my voice to a low plane, trying to rob it of any suggestion or overtone of aggressiveness.

Half an hour later Mr. Crane called me to his desk and questioned me closely about my schooling, about how much mathematics I had had. He seemed pleased when I told him that I had had two years of algebra.

"How would you like to learn this trade?" he asked.

"I'd like it fine, sir. I'd like nothing better," I said.

He told me that he wanted to train a Negro boy in the optical trade; he wanted to help him, guide him. I tried to answer in a way that would let him know that I would try to be worthy of what he was doing. He took me to the stenographer and said:

"This is Richard. He's going to be with us."

He then led me into the rear room of the office, which turned out to be a tiny factory filled with many strange machines smeared with red dust.

"Reynolds," he said to a young white man, "this is Richard."

"What you saying there, boy!" Reynolds grinned and boomed at me.

Mr. Crane took me to the older man.

"Pease, this is Richard, who'll work with us."

Pease looked at me and nodded. Mr. Crane then held forth to the two white men about my duties; he told them to break me in gradually to the workings of the shop, to instruct me in the mechanics of grinding and polishing lenses. They nodded their assent.

"Now, boy, let's see how clean you can get this place," Mr. Crane said.

"Yes, sir."

I swept, mopped, dusted, and soon had the office and the shop clean. In the afternoons, when I had caught up with my work, I ran errands. In an idle moment I would stand and watch the two white men grinding lenses on the machines. They said nothing to me and I said nothing to them. The first day passed, the second, the third, a week passed and I received my five dollars. A month passed. But I was not learning anything and nobody had volunteered to help me. One afternoon I walked up to Reynolds and asked him to tell me about the work.

"What are you trying to do, get smart, nigger?" he asked me.

"No, sir," I said.

I was baffled. Perhaps he just did not want to help me. I went to Pease, reminding him that the boss had said that I was to be given a chance to learn the trade.

"Nigger, you think you're white, don't you?"

"No, sir."

"You're acting mighty like it," he said.

"I was only doing what the boss told me to do," I said.

Pease shook his fist in my face.

"This is a *white* man's work around here," he said.

From then on they changed toward me; they said good morning no more. When I was just a bit slow in performing some duty, I was called a lazy black sonofabitch. I kept silent, striving to offer no excuse for worsening of relations. But one day Reynolds called me to his machine.

"Richard, how long is your thing?" he asked me.

"What thing?" I asked.

"You know what I mean," he said. "The thing the bull uses on the cow."

I turned away from him; I had heard that whites regarded Negroes as animals in sex matters and his words made me angry.

"I heard that a nigger can stick his prick in the ground and spin around on it like a top," he said, chuckling. "I'd like to see you do that. I'd give you a dime, if you did it."

I ignored him. Mr. Pease was watching me closely; then I saw them exchange glances. My job was not leading to what Mr. Crane had said it would. I had been humble, and now I was reaping the wages of humility.

"Come here, boy," Pease said.

I walked to his bench.

"You didn't like what Reynolds just said, did you?" he asked.

"Oh, it's all right," I said smiling.

"You didn't like it. I could see it on your face," he said.

I stared at him and backed away.

"Did you ever get into any trouble?" he asked.

"No, sir."

"What would you do if you got into trouble?"

"I don't know, sir."

"Well, watch yourself and don't get into trouble," he warned.

I wanted to report these clashes to Mr. Crane, but the thought of what Pease or Reynolds would do to me if they learned that I had "snitched" stopped me. I worked through the days and tried to hide my resentment under a nervous, cryptic smile.

The climax came at noon one summer day. Pease called me to his workbench; to get to him I had to go between two narrow benches and stand with my back against a wall.

"Richard, I want to ask you something," Pease began pleasantly, not looking up from his work.

"Yes, sir."

Reynolds came over and stood blocking the narrow passage between the benches; he folded his arms and stared at me solemnly. I looked from one to the other, sensing trouble. Pease looked up and spoke slowly, so there would be no possibility of my not understanding.

"Richard, Reynolds here tells me that you called me Pease," he said.

I stiffened. A void opened up in me. I knew that this was the showdown.

He meant that I had failed to call him Mr. Pease. I looked at Reynolds; he was gripping a steel bar in his hand. I opened my mouth to speak, to protest, to assure Pease that I had never called him simply *Pease,* and that I had never had any intention of doing so, when Reynolds grabbed me by the collar, ramming my head against a wall.

"Now, be careful, nigger," snarled Reynolds, baring his teeth. "I heard you call 'im *Pease*. And if you say you didn't, you're calling me a liar, see?" He waved the steel bar threateningly.

If I had said: No, sir, Mr. Pease, I never called you *Pease*, I would by inference have been calling Reynolds a liar; and if I had said: Yes, sir, Mr. Pease, I called you *Pease*, I would have been pleading guilty to the worst insult that a Negro can offer to a southern white man. I stood trying to think of a neutral course that would resolve this quickly risen nightmare, but my tongue would not move.

"Richard, I asked you a question!" Pease said. Anger was creeping into his voice.

"I don't remember calling you *Pease*, Mr. Pease," I said cautiously. "And if I did, I sure didn't mean...."

"You black sonofabitch! You called me *Pease*, then!" he spat, rising and slapping me till I bent sideways over a bench.

Reynolds was up on top of me demanding:

"Didn't you call him *Pease*? If you say you didn't, I'll rip your gut string loose with this f-k-g bar, you black granny dodger! You can't call a white man a liar and get away with it!"

I wilted. I begged them not to hit me. I knew what they wanted. They wanted me to leave the job.

"I'll leave," I promised. "I'll leave right now!"

They gave me a minute to get out of the factory, and warned me not to show up again or tell the boss. Reynolds loosened his hand on my collar and I ducked out of the room. I did not see Mr. Crane or the stenographer in the office. Pease and Reynolds had so timed it that Mr. Crane and the stenographer would be out when they turned on the terror. I went to the street and waited for the boss to return. I saw Griggs wiping glass shelves in the jewelry store and I beckoned to him. He came out and I told him what had happened.

"Then what are you standing there like a fool for?" he demanded. "Won't you ever learn? Get home! They might come down!"

I walked down Capitol Street feeling that the sidewalk was unreal, that I was unreal, that the people were unreal, yet expecting somebody to demand to know what right I had to be on the streets. My wound went deep; I felt that I had been slapped out of the human race. When I reached home, I did not tell the family what had happened; I merely told them that I had quit, that I was not making enough money, that I was seeking another job.

That night Griggs came to my house; we went for a walk.

"You got a goddamn tough break," he said.

"Can you say it was my fault?" I asked.

He shook his head.

"Well, what about your goddamn philosophy of meekness?" I asked him bitterly.

"These things just happen," he said, shrugging.

"They owe me money," I said.

"That's what I came about," he said. "Mr. Crane wants you to come in at ten in the morning. Ten sharp, now, mind you, because he'll be there and those guys won't gang up on you again."

The next morning at ten I crept up the stairs and peered into the office of the optical shop to make sure that Mr. Crane was in. He was at his desk. Pease and Reynolds were at their machines in the rear.

"Come in, Richard," Mr. Crane said.

I pulled off my hat and walked into the office; I stood before him.

"Sit down," he said.

I sat. He stared at me and shook his head.

"Tell me, what happened?"

An impulse to speak rose in me and died with the realization that I was facing a wall that I would never breach. I tried to speak several times and could make no sounds. I grew tense and tears burnt my cheeks.

"Now, just keep control of yourself," Mr. Crane said.

I clenched my fists and managed to talk.

"I tried to do my best here," I said.

"I believe you," he said. "But I want to know what happened. Which one bothered you?"

"Both of 'em," I said.

Reynolds came running to the door and I rose. Mr. Crane jumped to his feet.

"Get back in there," he told Reynolds.

"That nigger's lying!" Reynolds said. "I'll kill 'im if he lies on me!"

"Get back in there or get out," Mr. Crane said.

Reynolds backed away, keeping his eyes on me.

"Go ahead," Mr. Crane said. "Tell me what happened."

Then again I could not speak. What could I accomplish by telling him? I was black; I lived in the South. I would never learn to operate those machines as long as those two white men in there stood by them. Anger and fear welled in me as I felt what I had missed; I leaned forward and clapped my hands to my face.

"No, no, now," Mr. Crane said. "Keep control of yourself. No matter what happens, keep control ..."

"I know," I said in a voice not my own. "There's no use of my saying anything."

"Do you want to work here?" he asked me.

I looked at the white faces of Pease and Reynolds; I imagined their waylaying me, killing me....

"No, sir," I breathed.

"Why?"

"I'm scared," I said. "They would kill me."

Mr. Crane turned and called Pease and Reynolds into the office.

"Now, tell me which one bothered you. Don't be afraid. Nobody's going to hurt you," Mr. Crane said.

I stared ahead of me and did not answer. He waved the men inside. The white stenographer looked at me with wide eyes and I felt drenched in shame, naked to my soul. The whole of my being felt violated, and I knew that my own fear had helped to violate it. I was breathing hard and struggling to master my feelings.

"Can I get my money, sir?" I asked at last.

"Just sit a minute and take hold of yourself," he said.

I waited and my roused senses grew slowly calm.

"I'm awfully sorry about this," he said.

"I had hoped for a lot from this job," I said. "I'd wanted to go to school, to college..."

"I know," he said. "But what are you going to do now?"

My eyes traveled over the office, but I was not seeing.

"I'm going away," I said.

"What do you mean?"

"I'm going to get out of the South," I breathed.

"Maybe that's best," he said. "I'm from Illinois. Even for me, it's hard here. I can do just so much."

He handed me my money, more than I had earned for the week. I thanked him and rose to leave. He rose. I went into the hallway and he followed me. He reached out his hand.

"It's tough for you down here," he said.

I barely touched his hand. I walked swiftly down the hall, fighting against crying again. I ran down the steps, then paused and looked back up. He was standing at the head of the stairs, shaking his head. I went into the sunshine and walked home like a blind man.

Sue Sumii: Readings from *The River with No Bridge*

Excerpts from Sue Sumii, *The River with No Bridge*, trans. Susan Wilkerson. Boston: Charles E. Tuttle, 1989.

Introduction

The River with No Bridge was published in six volumes between the years 1961 and 1973. The work draws upon the experience of Burakumin people between 1908 and 1924 in Nara, Japan, and has been popular in Japan.

The translator has provided a particularly evocative description of the book. "The six volumes mirror the development of the awareness of the Burakumin of their rights and dignity as human beings."[1] As in many forms of Japanese fiction, the focus is on events that took place during this period: the death of Emperor Meiji, the rice riots, the massacre of Koreans in Tokyo after the great Kanto earthquake in 1923. The first volume traces the maturation of a child, Koji, whose growing sense of the injustice of the system derives not only from the prejudice he meets from other children and the teachers at school, but also from what he is taught. The purpose of education in pre-war Japan was to train children to become docile and loyal citizens.

While the discrimination that occurs in *The River with No Bridge* is based on actual experiences, Koji's views of the world are those of Sue Sumii. Although not a Burakumin, she was brought up in the same area of Nara Prefecture in which the novel is set and, like Koji, was six years old in 1908.

Insight afforded Sue Sumii enabled her to see that the veneration of the sacred and the rejection of the despised are really two sides of the same coin. She wrote: "No one is born more than a human being/No one is born less than a human being.[2]"

Plot Summary

Sue Sumii's six-volume saga based on the Burakumin struggle to escape prejudice and discrimination focuses on the lives of the residents of Komori, a Buraku village in Nara Prefecture in central Japan. The novel traces the maturation of a central symbolic figure, Koji, a bright and sensitive child who comes face-to-face with discrimination as a member of a despised and stigmatized minority. As he passes from childhood to manhood, he experiences name calling, teasing, bullying, and raw prejudice from students and teachers alike. As he grows older, he faces the limitations of life as a Burakumin—confinement to low-status trades, for example, the making of sandals and glue; being cheated by unscrupulous traders; enduring continuous discrimination by members of surrounding communities; and heartbreaking relationships with people outside the Burakumin community. As he enters manhood, he discovers Suiheisha, a political organization dedicated to elevating the status of Burakumin, and adopts their manifesto: "The time has come to be proud of our heritage."

---

1 Sue Sumii, *The River with No Bridge*, trans. Susan Wilkerson (Boston: Charles E. Tuttle, 1990), 7.

2 Ibid., xi–xiv.

Reading 5

(pages 29–36)

The children at Sakata Primary School had also finished lunch and were now gathering round Senkichi Sayama in the playground. He was the center of attention because of the "magic glasses" hanging round his neck. A few children had already been allowed to peep through them and, in high spirits, were loudly boasting:

"I could see all the trees and paths on Miminashi Hill as if they were right next to the school. They're a soldier's binoculars. But only the top soldiers have binoculars like that. And I had a look through them!"

"I saw some people threshing. And the thresher, too; they were so clear."

"I saw a factory chimney. I almost jumped seeing it so near."

"Well, I saw an oxcart. The ox lifted up its tail and dropped ox dung. Ha, ha, ha!"

"Fibber!"

"I am not. It did drop ox dung."

"Idiot. Of course an ox drops ox dung!"

Everybody roared with laughter and in the midst of the merriment, Senkichi shouted out, "All those who want to look through my binoculars must line up and wait their turn."

The children formed a long line behind Senkichi and, rather hesitantly, Koji joined the end. He noticed Seitaro standing some distance away from them. "Maybe Seitaro doesn't want to look through the magic glasses," he thought, feeling sorry that his brother would miss such a treat.

The binoculars passed from child to child down the line under the supervision of Senkichi's best friend, Shigeo Iwase. The children were still in a state of excitement over the Maneuvers and, led by Senkichi, they started to chatter about rifles and machine guns, scouts and buglers, and eventually the soldiers who should have been quartered with them, at which point the talk grew even more animated.

"Four soldiers were meant to stay with us and we'd got all new mattresses and pillows made. Then we felt like idiots when it suddenly turned out they weren't coming."

"They said five soldiers were coming to stay at our place, and then they said they couldn't 'cause they were losing the battle, and they all went away."

"Some officers were quartered with us and so we'd bought heaps of fish and beef, and a great barrel of saké. But there's no time to eat when you're losing a battle, and now we've got to finish it all by ourselves. We'll be stuffing ourselves forever!"

"Ha, ha! It's no good being on the losing side."

"It's bad enough in the Maneuvers, but it's even worse in a real war."

"Only the Russians and Chinese lose in a real war."

They all laughed again.

But Seitaro, who was still standing apart from the rest, neither spoke nor laughed. He was not alone in being silent; none of the children from Komori had anything to say because none of the soldiers had been quartered with their families.

Senkichi Sayama caught sight of Seitaro. "It's all right for Sei and the others from Komori, isn't it? They've got nothing to worry about. They couldn't care less if the soldiers lost and went away because there was never any chance of them staying with them."

"That's right."

It was not Seitaro who answered back but Shigemi Nagai, one of Tosaku Nagai's daughters and Natsu's younger sister. At school she was known as "Hachimero," which could mean a tomboy or, more harshly, a hussy.

Shigemi paused and looked around quickly at her Komori friends before continuing, "We couldn't put them up in Komori because we're all poor. We don't have any spare mattresses and we can't afford to buy nice things to eat. But Sei's family steamed some sweet potatoes for the soldiers camping on the riverbank. You lot didn't give them anything to eat, did you, even though they were meant to stay with you. We did a lot more for them in Komori."

"What! Sweet potatoes!" shrieked Senkichi, and all the others collapsed with laughter.

Seitaro felt as if he had been knocked over. "They're all laughing at me," he thought. "They're laughing at me because I'm poor. 'We bought heaps of saké and fish but you only had sweet potatoes'—that's what they're saying. The soldiers were pleased with them though. They even patted Koji and me on the head."

Wanting to explain this to the other children, he mustered up courage and spoke quickly:

"The soldiers camping out enjoyed having some nice hot potatoes on such a cold night."

"Those soldiers are from the Nagoya division," said Senkichi, speaking with deliberate slowness. "They don't know these parts. D'you think they'd have eaten the potatoes if they'd known you're from Komori? On top of losing the battle, the poor things ended up eating *eta* potatoes! Stinking *eta* potatoes!" and he held his nose, pretending to vomit.

It was Toyota Matsuzaki's turn to have the binoculars. "I don't want a look," he said, pushing the binoculars away and stepping out of the line.

"Well, why bother to wait your turn then?" Shigeo's tone of voice and stance clearly showed his annoyance at Toyota's rebuff.

"We don't have to lend them to anybody who doesn't want a look," snapped Senkichi, glaring at Toyota.

"I don't know what he's got to be so stuck up about. What's so special about a pair of old field glasses?" Toyota gripped Seitaro's shoulder. "Come on, Sei, let's go."

"Ha, ha! Look, one's an *eta* and the other's a bastard. Just right for each other, they both stink!"

Senkichi was suddenly punched in the chest, and the next moment a full-scale fight had broken out.

"Teacher, they're fighting! Teacher, they're fighting!"

"Teacher, teacher, the *eta* are making trouble!"

Word of the fight soon reached the staff room, upsetting the midday calm.

VII

The wooden storm doors at the front of the house facing the road were all closed and inside there was semi-darkness. Koji slid open the screen doors of the work-room and sat down there. Across the narrow backyard where the washing was hung out to dry, the door of a makeshift shed was wide open, revealing a straw mat, a winnower, an old sack, some bundles of straw, and, in the corner, a mortar for polishing rice. A stillness lay over these objects as if they were aware of their owners' absence.

Tick-tock, tick-tock, tick-tock—Koji glanced at the clock; it was nearly three. "Seitaro'll be back at three," he said in a small voice, not really believing it. "Seitaro'll be back at three," he repeated a little louder. But it became increasingly obvious that his brother would not be back by then.

"They dragged him off to the staff room all covered in dirt from the play-ground and the teacher hit him when he kept on struggling. No, he won't come back at three." Koji's face suddenly contorted and the tears streamed down his cheeks.

Presently, he reached inside his toy box and brought out some shell spinning-tops. His fingers were still damp from wiping away his tears, which helped him to wind them up more neatly than usual. When satisfied, he let one go. It was a good throw and the top spun smoothly with a whirring noise. Koji quickly wound up the next and set the two tops spinning together.

"Keep going, Sei, keep going. Keep going, Toyo."

The third was bright red. Koji spun it full of confidence but, as if it were angry, the top flew through the air and hit the door. Koji wound the lifeline again.

"Come on, keep going!" The top whirled round smartly this time. "Shige, don't give up. Please don't give up."

Koji was playing in deadly earnest: the red top really was "Hachimero."

Ding, ding, ding. The clock chimed three. Koji strained his ears; he could hear people talking in the distance. Maybe Seitaro was among them.

He ran out to the front of the house. Seven or eight children, with a purple flag in their midst, were following the path as it curved toward Komori; and Seitaro was not among them. Koji swallowed hard, fighting the feeling of panic which gripped him. He started to walk toward the flag.

"Sei's been made to stand holding the buckets, Ko."

"He won't be back for ages yet."

"Not before dark."

Did they care at all, Koji wondered as the children surrounded him. He glared at his brother's friends and then pushed his way out of the group and sped like the wind toward school.

Sei's been made to stand holding those buckets, he thought. Those heavy buckets full of water!

The weight of them distorted Koji's face.

Seitaro almost fell to his knees again and again, giving way under the weight of the buckets, but each time he caught sight of the Headmaster he braced himself once more. The Headmaster, who was in charge of the fifth grade, had handed down the punishment himself.

"You may not put the buckets down until you understand that you should not have hit Senkichi Sayama and until you show that you are truly sorry for what you have done," he repeated several times.

Even if it meant standing there all night, even if his arms were pulled out of their sockets, Seitaro was determined to go on holding the buckets, and he felt sure that Toyota was equally resolved. But the color was draining from Toyota's face, second by second, and he had almost reached the limits of his endurance.

As if he could not bear to stand back and watch, Mr. Egawa, the senior teacher, called out to them, "Don't be so obstinate both of you. Hurry up and apologize. After all, you shouldn't have hit Sayama."

"No, leave them. They obviously still think they are in the right. We must knock some sense into them."

However, no sooner had the Headmaster uttered these words than Mr. Egawa went over to the two boys. "Hatanaka." He put his hand on Seitaro's shoulder.

Seitaro felt tears welling up in his eyes. The touch of that hand brought happy memories of his first year at school flooding back: Mr. Egawa had been his teacher then and had often quietly placed his hand on Seitaro's head or shoulder.

"Put the buckets down."

The order was gently given and the two boys lowered their buckets. At once, a cold sensation shot through their shoulders, followed immediately by a tingling in their fingers; they had been delivered from humiliation and the blood was coursing through the veins of their arms once more.

"Apologize to the Headmaster." Mr. Egawa put his hand on Toyota's shoulder. "He has business to attend to and must be leaving now. Hurry up and apologize and then you can go home at once. Your mother's bound to be worried about you."

"But I haven't done anything wrong, sir." Toyota addressed his remark to the Headmaster rather than Mr. Egawa.

"What do you mean you've done nothing wrong! Do you think it is all right to hurt Sayama?"

The Headmaster had just put on his hat but now he snatched it off and flung it down on the table. The three other teachers who were working in the staff room pretended not to be aware of what was going on.

"Sir, it was me who hit Sen," cried Seitaro so loudly he even startled himself. At the same time, Toyota unexpectedly picked up both the buckets again.

The Headmaster took this as a personal affront.

"Well, if that's the way you feel, you can stand there until the morning," he roared, sweeping out of the room.

"Put down those buckets and stop being so stubborn," said Mr. Egawa. "Now, it seems that when Sayama refused to show you his binoculars, you both got angry and hit him. If that's really what happened then you are both in the wrong, aren't you?"

"That's not how it was, sir, that's a lie. The Headmaster only believes Sen, but Sen said rude things about us."

"I see. Well, you'd better tell me all about it right from the beginning. The other teachers will listen as well. What started the fight?"

"Sweet potatoes."

The lady teacher sniggered discreetly but the other two, who were young men, laughed outright.

"Well, what happened?"

"He said they stank. They stank 'cause they were *eta* potatoes."

The teachers stopped working and looked at each other.

"Then you hit Sayama?" continued Mr. Egawa, after a moment's pause. His low voice sounded tense.

"Yes, that's right. Sen's always calling me an *eta*. Some of the others do, too. Sir, I hate being called that more than anything. And it's not something I can change, however hard I try. Please tell me what I can do about it, sir, please."

"Yes, I see. I understand only too well, now. And Matsuzaki, you got angry because your friend, Hatanaka, had been insulted."

"Yes," Toyota began, but then he closed his mouth: naturally he had hit Senkichi because of Seitaro but, even more, on his own account. He had been called a bastard; and that was not something he could help, any more than Seitaro could help being an *eta*. Nevertheless, he had been abused as if he were ugly; tormented as if he were evil; and when that happened all he could do was hit back. His grip on the buckets tightened.

"For goodness sake put them down. I understand everything and tomorrow I'll explain it all to the Headmaster."

Mr. Egawa wrenched the buckets from Toyota's hands and took them outside.

"Now hurry along home; it will soon be dark."

"Yes, sir."

Toyota and Seitaro both bowed and the three teachers all gave a slight nod back. Then they rushed to the school gates where they drew together for a moment. "Toyo," said Seitaro, "Sei," said Toyota; and they ran off in opposite directions.

"Seitaro!"

It could not be, so late...Yet there was no doubt that it was Koji who came scampering like a puppy toward him from the shadow of the riverbank.

"Koji, you mustn't tell Mom or Gran about this."

"No."

And not another word was spoken. The evening breeze played with the hems of their kimonos as they crossed over to the west side of Ohashi Bridge.

VIII

"You're very late, aren't you?" Fudé stared at Seitaro suspiciously. She and Nui had just arrived back from the field with the baskets of rice.

"I was busy after school."

Seitaro handed his bundle of books to Koji and helped his mother and grandmother unload the baskets.

"That's all right then. I was afraid you'd got into trouble and been kept in."

"Well, I didn't."

Nui smiled. "There's nothing so terrible about misbehaving and getting into a fight, so long as you don't come home blubbering about it. Boys will be boys, and you can't be playing with dolls, can you, Seitaro?"

Nevertheless, Nui felt secretly worried about him. "Something's the matter. I know something's happened," she thought, impatient to find out what it might be.

Reading 6

(pages 36–39)

That evening, Fudé lit the fire to heat up a bath. It was the first time for many days and she was longing for one, especially after work like threshing, which left her covered in white dust from head to foot, even her eyelashes. But when Seitaro and Koji had had theirs, she invited the neighbors round for one, too, as was usual in the village, and waited her turn until the very last.

Seitaro and Koji completely forgot their tiredness and stayed up, sitting by the lamp. Their nearest neighbors, a couple who lived on the north side, also lingered by the brazier as if they had been asked round for the evening—which was understandable, since the only chance they had to enjoy themselves and indulge in some lively gossip was once or twice a month when they got together with the other villagers for a bath. Fortunately, the husband, Hirokichi Shimura, not only had the gift of the gab but a constant supply of stories as well. He worked as a carrier and traveled far and wide, sometimes pulling a cart laden with goods right into the heart of the Yoshino mountains, or to Osaka and back.

Tonight, Hirokichi waited for Fudé to finish her bath before opening his mouth and revealing a set of yellow, tobacco-stained teeth.

"I heard a good one today," he began.

"Tell it to us over a cup of tea," said Fudé, feeling sociable.

"Oh, don't bother," Hirokichi's wife, Kané, waved her hand. "It's not worth making him a cup of tea; you never know what he's talking about half the time. If he gets tired of talking, a glass of water will do."

"Now I ask you, what's a fine man like myself doing married to such a cold-hearted woman," cried Hirokichi in high spirits.

"Talk about a happy couple: What's happened to this story we're all dying to hear?" Nui, too, seemed to have quite forgotten her weariness.

"Well, now," Hirokichi slapped his knees, "it is with great trepidation that I announce the following story is about His Majesty, the Emperor. I'm sure you and Koji know that the Emperor came to the Maneuvers, Seitaro. Well, some fella picked up His Imperial Majesty's stub ends. What a find!"

"Where did he find them?" asked Seitaro, his eyes shining.

"That I couldn't tell you, but it must be somewhere around Miminashi Hill."

"But stub ends aren't any use."

"Now that's where you're wrong; you obviously don't realize their real worth. These are stub ends marked with the Imperial seal and graciously left by His Majesty. They're cigarettes that have been in the Emperor's mouth and you won't find anything like them no matter how hard you look. The fella that picked them up has really hit the jackpot. He'll treasure them like a family heirloom. Anyway, this other man, that lives nearby, heard about it and he decided he wanted a keepsake of His Majesty, too. So off he went to the hill to have a look round but there wasn't any more stub ends. So he used his brains and...hee, hee,...what d'you think he found, Sei?"

"Footprints."

Fudé, Nui, and Kané burst out laughing at the thought of the man trying to take home a footprint.

Hirokichi paused and then said, "Well, it seems he did take back a keepsake."

"He scraped up the soil the footprints was in," scoffed his wife.

Hirokichi shook his head. "With *your* brains you'll never guess; I'll have to tell you. He found the Emperor's crap. He's a smart fella all right."

They were all taken aback.

Hirokichi continued in an increasingly exultant tone of voice. "The Emperor spent a day and a night at Miminashi Hill and this fella was sharp enough to realize that even His Majesty has to crap."

"Even a *kami*?" asked Koji in a small voice, staring up at the family *kamidana*, the altar to the guardian spirits of the household, above the doorway leading into the bedroom. Hirokichi's story was incomprehensible to him: he could not even imagine the teachers at school crapping like everybody else, much less the Emperor, who was meant to be a *kami*.

Nui and Fudé were overcome with mirth.

"I've heard of the Water-Fetching ceremony at Nara's Nigatsudo, but this is the first time I've ever heard of the Crap-Fetching ceremony on Miminashi Hill," said Kané, wiping away tears of laughter.

Seitaro silently shook himself; there was so much he wanted to say he did not know where to begin.

With his pipe in his mouth, Hirokichi added, "Funny what a difference there is between people when we're all the same human beings. There they are, treating the Emperor's crap like treasure, but in our case, they think even the rice we grow is dirty and stinks." He raised his eyes to the ceiling.

Seitaro gave a start and then froze: maybe Hirokichi had heard about the trouble at school; maybe he was hinting at the sweet potatoes when he talked about their rice stinking.

"Koji, let's turn in now. It's half past nine already," he urged.

Koji shook his head, showing a stubbornness unusual for him. "I'm not a bit sleepy. I want to listen to some more stories."

Seitaro grew increasingly nervous. He was afraid Koji might blab about what had happened that day and he wanted to shield his mother and grandmother from the hopeless pain of the jibe about "stinking potatoes."

Koji leaned toward Hirokichi. "Uncle, what's a bastard?"

"A bastard? What are you talking about?"

"It's about a person."

"A person?"

"Yes, I heard one boy call another boy a bastard."

"Ah, I've got you now. I bet the one who was called that went red."

Koji made no reply.

"Or did he get angry? They usually do. A bastard's a child who hasn't got a father."

"Are me and Seitaro bastards then?"

There was another explosion of laughter. Fudé tapped Koji on the shoulder.

"You've got a father, Koji."

"No, I haven't. He's dead."

"Yes, but he was alive when you were little. The boy who's a bastard never had a father right from the start."

"Yes, he has. Toyo said his father in Osaka sent him that book with the red cover," retorted Seitaro, unable to remain silent.

"Ha, ha. He's too much for me. I'm blessed if I can answer that one. We'd better be off." Hirokichi stretched himself, twisting his hips from side to side, and stepped down to the *doma*.

"But if a bastard's out of the top drawer, it doesn't matter, of course," he suddenly remarked as he looked for his straw sandals. "That Yanagihara, for instance—the lady-in-waiting of the second rank or whatever they call her—she's no more than the Emperor's concubine really. But her son's the Crown Prince, isn't he? In the old days, all the lords had twenty or thirty concubines, the shogun more like fifty, and all them concubines' sons was important samurai. Not like us. Our kids are always looked down on, legitimate or not. We stink, same as our rice."

"Don't talk such rubbish! We've just had a good bath, haven't we?" Kané laughed and went out just ahead of her husband.

"All right, all right." Hirokichi trotted after her.

Fudé and her family felt dazed for a moment as if a whirlwind had swept out. Nui broke the silence:

"Seitaro, did you play with this Toyo today?"

"Yes. I went over to Toyo's."

"What's his mother like?"

"Very pretty."

Seitaro escaped to the bedroom.

"I wonder if he did play there." Nui looked at Fudé with a suspicious expression on her face.

Fudé was staring vacantly at the lamp, not yet recovered from the whirlwind. "Our rice stinks. Our children stink," she thought, the words sinking down inside her like sediment.

Reading 7

(pages 99–104)

The house at Ino was not particularly large, with no more than four rooms—an eight-mat, a six-mat, and two four-and-a-half-mat—but its high white gables looked down on the roofs of the neighboring houses, and the front of the rice storehouse, next to the shed, was decorated with a black-and-white pattern, giving it an air of prosperity. At the back of the house, too, there was a roofed well, with a pulley and a thick hemp rope, where it was possible to draw water without getting wet on rainy days. This well caught Koji's fancy more than anything else at his grandfather's.

As he pulled the rope, he suddenly remembered the times children from other villages had jeered at him—"Look at that poor good-for-nothing *eta*." "I wonder if they're all *eta* at Grandad's," he thought. "Master Hidé, the priest's son, said all the relatives of Komori people are *eta* too, but they look well-off here. There's a gateway, a tiled roof, a storehouse, and a well with a pulley."

Soshichi noticed his grandson pulling the well rope and came hurrying out anxiously onto the veranda. "Take care you don't slip, Koji," he called.

"I will," replied his grandson meekly.

Soshichi did not have any favorites among his grandchildren, but he felt a particular concern for Seitaro and Koji because their father had been killed in the war; and of the two, he felt closest to Koji, whose face was the image of Fudé's.

Koji gulped some water and then, wiping his mouth, returned to his place by the brazier. Chié stepped down into the *doma* and busied herself preparing the afternoon meal—in this region, it was the custom to have four meals a day, including one in the middle of the afternoon. Nanaé followed her mother, hovering about the sink and stove, and Koji and his grandfather were left alone in the room.

Soshichi stared at his grandson, still gripped by the feeling of unease and apprehension that had overtaken him a few moments before. "I wonder if the other children at school make him cry, too, with names like *eta* and Four-Fingers. And even if he doesn't suffer much from that sort of thing now, while he's still only a child, I expect he'll have a hard time of it when he's a bit older," he thought; but he pretended to smile and said cheerfully, "You've got a bright future ahead of you, Koji, with your love of books."

Koji stared silently at one of the pages of Keizo's storybook.

"Don't you think so?" pressed his grandfather.

"What, Grandad?"

"I said you've got a bright future, with your love of books. Would you like to study to be a teacher?"

Koji did not reply.

"Don't you want to be a teacher?"

"Yes, I do."

"Well then, that's what you'd better do."

"I can't, Grandad."

"Why not?"

"We're poor good-for-nothings." A bitter little smile crossed Koji's young face, at the sight of which his grandfather felt a sharp pang: it showed that Koji was already aware of himself as an *eta*. Soshichi wanted to weep unrestrainedly; he wanted to face the invisible enemy that was trying to crush them as *eta* and strike out at such hatred with all his might. At the same time, he needed no one to tell him how utterly futile that would be.

"Ha, ha, ha.... So you're poor good-for-nothings, are you?" he laughed, with tears in his eyes—his way of avoiding a collision with the *eta* wall confronting him. Now sixty-five, he still did not really understand why they were what they were. Not that he was illiterate: on the contrary, he was one of the most educated men in Ino, with the result that his thinking was permeated with Confucian ideas, such as "Heaven cannot support two suns, nor earth two masters." He believed that as long as one sun shone in the heavens, it was quite natural for there to be one sovereign ruler in the land, supported by a glittering array of officials and dignitaries. The only aspect of this scheme that he could not figure out was why there were people like themselves despised as *eta*. Why did there have to be *eta* at all? He had resigned himself to being one by thinking that it must be his karma; but this was merely a form of self-deception to make life bearable. Moreover, he himself realized this; at heart, he did not really believe in such ideas as predestination. Stroking the edge of the brazier, he said, "But there are families much poorer than yours, Koji. And poverty's nothing to be afraid of. If you work hard enough, you're bound to do well in the end."

"Were you poor to start with, Grandad?"

"We certainly were. Not that we're all that well-off now."

"Yes, you are. You've a storehouse and a gateway, like well-to-do people have."

"You'll soon be building a gateway and a storehouse at your home, too."

"No, we won't."

"Why not?"

"We live in Komori."

Soshichi was taken aback.

"Grandad, Komori's an *eta* village."

"Who said a thing like that?"

"Other people do. They all do."

There was silence.

"Grandad, what is an *eta*?"

"I don't know myself," replied Soshichi, shaking his head vigorously. Koji looked down: he felt that his grandfather had shaken his head to admonish him never to mention the word *eta* again.

"It's true what Master Hidé said," he thought. "All the relatives of Komori people are *eta*. Grandad's family, too, even though they look so well-off. That's why he's angry and doesn't want me to talk about it again."

He turned over the pages of the book, pretending to read. Presently, Nanaé came to tell them that the meal was ready.

"It doesn't look as if the troops are coming yet. I think I'll join Koji and start without them," Soshichi said, settling down beside his grandson. As a special treat, there was a bowl heaped with white rice on the small tray before each of them.

They were still eating when the sound of the troops' triumphant return reached their ears. Each was singing a different song:

"Defending or attacking, the iron battleship..."
"With a thousand miles before us..."
"Our country is so far away..."

When they caught sight of the trays for the afternoon meal, however, they revealed their true colors and with one voice, cried, "Oh, I'm starving!"

Seitaro was carrying the Ichimatsu doll with the long-sleeved red kimono. He had been playing the part of the white horse on which Jeanne d'Arc rode, but now that the battle was over he suddenly felt embarrassed and quickly undid the cord that tied the doll to his back. Chié went behind him and deftly caught it.

"Yaé's tired, Nanaé, you'd better put her to bed soon."

Nanaé immediately spread a small mattress in a corner of the room and lay down beside her doll.

Sleep, little one, sleep,
Be good and don't cry;
Sleep, little one, sleep.
Mommy will hug you
And kiss you good night.

An atmosphere of quiet and peace stole over the room, and Soshichi looked the soul of contentment.

All at once, the calm was shattered as Nanaé started screaming. Koji was so startled he could not say a word.

"Whatever is it? Has a wasp stung you?" asked Soshichi and tried to pick her up.

Nanaé pushed him away. "My doll! My doll!"

"What's the matter with your doll?"

"She's lost her thumb!"

They all put down their chopsticks in surprise. Chié rushed over to Nanaé and picked up the doll.

"Oh dear, so it has," she sighed. Sadly, the doll's right thumb had been knocked off.

"Put it back! Quick, put it back! Put her thumb back!" cried Nanaé again and again between sobs.

"There, there, I'll put it back for you. There's no need to cry so," said her grandfather, and walking over to the family shrine at the back of the room, he took down the present of *manju* buns which had been placed there as an offering.

"Here you are, Nanaé, here's a red *manju*. You can have as many as you want." Chié desperately tried to soothe her daughter.

But Nanaé continued to crouch on the floor sobbing, "I don't want one. I don't want a *manju*. Put my doll's thumb back!"

Seitaro did not know what to say in apology: although of course he had damaged the doll quite unwittingly, there was no denying that he was to blame; nor that the dainty little hand now had only four fingers.

Soshichi stood there sorrowfully, his arms folded. "Throw it away. I'll buy you a much better one," he said after a while.

Nanaé sprang up immediately. Her grandfather was staring at her sternly, as if he might take the doll from her at any moment.

"You mustn't. You mustn't throw her away." Clutching the doll, Nanaé rushed over to Koji, who now seemed the best person to help since her grandfather was always singing his praises.

Soshichi's expression softened. "Stop crying then and play with Koji. I'll give you some *manju* to share with your doll."

He gave each of the five children two buns, one white and one red. Keizo started munching them at once, but Ken'ichi slipped his into the breast of his kimono and dashed out of the back door. Seitaro ran after him.

"I'm not going to play soldiers anymore, Sei."

"I'm too tired even if I wanted to."

"You did fight well today."

"That's 'cause the commanding officer's so good."

"Are you really going to be a soldier, Sei?"

"Yeah. Anyway, you have to join up, like it or not, if you pass the test," replied Seitaro, assuming an air of authority.

"It's tough being a soldier, though."

"I don't care."

"The commanding officer's orders are *our* orders. Know what that means?"

"Course I do," said Seitaro, dispatching a red *manju* in two bites.

Beyond the shed there was some wasteland, in a corner of which stood two persimmon trees, leaning over slightly. On the other side was a path, which ran between cultivated fields.

Ken'ichi shinnied up one of the persimmon trees, sat down on a branch, and brought out his *manju*. "You bought them at that cake shop in Iwase, didn't you? This pine spray is their mark."

"You don't miss much, do you?"

Seitaro also climbed up the tree and brought out his remaining white bun; as Ken'ichi had said, there was a pine-spray trademark on it.

"I'll come with you as far as there when you leave."

"You don't have to," said Seitaro earnestly; he intended to pass the shop as quickly as possible and did not want to have to say goodbye there.

"Sounds as if Nanaé's stopped crying," remarked Ken'ichi presently. "A couple of *manju* and the crybaby's laughing again. It's awful when she starts howling, though."

"It's my fault. It's no use crying over spilt milk, but I wish I'd been more careful. I was charging about like mad, like a good horse, and the doll's thumb must've caught on a branch and broken off."

"It doesn't matter. It's a wound of honor. Anyway, the real Jeanne d'Arc had a much worse time of it."

"But..."

Seitaro glanced quickly at Ken'ichi and a feeling of doubt crept over him. "Doesn't he mind at all? Doesn't it bother him it's only got four fingers now? I bet he'd be upset if he'd been called Four-Fingers, like I have," he thought; but he could not bring himself to talk about it. He hastily clambered down the tree, brushing against the new buds.

On returning to the house, they found Nanaé in the best of spirits, carrying her doll on her back. Now that Koji had tied a bandage around the damaged hand, she was fonder than ever of Yaé, much to the relief of Seitaro and Ken'ichi.

Kenkichi Sakai: "Having Excrement Thrown over Me"

"Having Excrement Thrown over Me" by Kenkichi Sakai (Head of Education & Policy Division, B.L.L., Izumi Branch). From *Burakumin Liberation News*, March, 1987.

Reading 8

Since I was around seven or eight years old, I realized there had been discrimination against my Buraku. So I then thought of running away from it as soon as possible. I entered the higher course of the High Elementary School but dropped out after only two months. Turning to my aunt in Nishinari area of Osaka for support, I got out of the village. I was thirteen at the time.

I worked for a shoemaker. But I was fired for something. While I was loafing around, I got to know a schoolgirl from Tesukayama Jogakuen High School. She was the daughter of a lumber dealer. When her parents found out she was pregnant, they got their servants to track down my lodgings. They took me behind the lumber dealer's house, violently beat and kicked me, and even threw excrement over me. Their final blow was to say, "Do you know where you come from? Stick to being an Eta and don't lay a hand on the daughter! Even if we kill you, we won't be guilty of any crime."

At the time I felt that what they said was right. "Since I am one of those human beings called 'Eta' whom people discriminate against," I thought, "whatever they do to me, I am not even 'qualified' to complain." When I was small, I was often teased with words like this: "Touch your ass! There's a tail there!" I thought it was true and actually touched my behind. I came across my coccyx. I didn't know that everybody had one and thought that only Burakumin possessed it. So I got it into my head that we were after all a different kind of human being. This flashed through my mind and I never considered confronting my persecutors. After being thrown outside, I was walking along just as I was, covered with excrement, when a policeman asked, "What happened?" I told him my story. "It's unpardonable," he exclaimed. "I'll go and make them apologize to you. Wait outside the house." He then went into the lumber dealer's place. However, several minutes later, it was my turn to be severely scolded: "Hey! You deceived the girl. You are worse than them."

After washing my body at a tap, I took the train to Shinodayama Station. I drifted around in utter misery and was about to kill myself by diving under a train. But a gateman at a railroad crossing noticed what I was trying to do and held me back. When I got back home, my mother said, "Wherever you go, you're in an impossible situation (i.e., you can't escape discrimination). Stay here and just do as I say." "You're the one who's to blame," I shot back. "You gave birth to me. If I had been born in a different family, I wouldn't have to go through all this." My sister remembers our exchange even now and says, "How could you say such things?" But it was true enough that I did feel bitter about my own mother. Only now can I imagine how my mother must have suffered after hearing those words from her own son's mouth. I am now sixty-one. But that episode of long ago comes to mind just as if it were something that happened yesterday.

Susumu Yamamoto: "My Experiences of Discrimination"

"My Experiences of Discrimination" by Susumu Yamamoto (Executive Staff, B.L.L., Osaka, Chief Secretary, Naniwa Branch). From *Burakumin Liberation News*, November, 1991.

Reading 9

I haven't had any experience of being directly discriminated against so far. I can say, though, that the whole forty-three years of my life have been nothing but discrimination.

I was born in Osaka. When I was little, we lost our family home as a result of the so-called Osaka Air Raid during the Pacific War and we moved to Nara. We had little to eat and malnutrition deprived me of my sight. I hardly have any vision in my left eye even now. The war hit most people hard, especially the Buraku people, who were forced to live at the bottom of society. My left eye is living testimony to the cruelty of discrimination and the war.

Later, my family returned to Osaka when I started to go to elementary school. When I look at a picture from that time, I can see only one child wearing a pair of shoes while everyone else is barefoot. Most of them were from Buraku, which meant that they were too poor to buy shoes or other everyday necessities. I myself was one of them. I had to stay home on rainy days because I didn't have an umbrella.

When I was a senior at junior high school, I couldn't pay the fee for the school trip. My teacher told me to get welfare support to cover the fee. The way the teacher behaved made me feel inferior because of my poverty and I started cutting classes after that.

At the school, no one questioned the discrimination method of education in those days. The students who planned to go on to higher education after graduation were the center of attention while students who intended to work were neglected by their teachers. I and most of my friends from the Buraku were in the latter group. Less than 10 percent of them were able to go to high school.

After graduating from a junior high, I changed my job several times. When I was employed as a shoemaker, the hard work caused a lung disease. Although I needed to be hospitalized, my financial circumstances did not permit me to lie down to make a complete recovery. I simply had to work to make a living. I know many tubercular patients in Buraku endured similar hardship. I now know that it was the result of discrimination.

I was soon unable to continue such hard work. After changing my job several more times, I encountered the liberation movement and I was "saved."

I lost my parents when I was very young, which meant that there was nobody to teach me the importance of learning—until I discovered the movement. So I can say now that education is the most important thing for Buraku Liberation and I will continue to learn and live for it.

Sandra Cisneros: Readings from *The House on Mango Street*

Selections from *The House on Mango Street,* Sandra Cisneros. New York: Vintage Books, A Division of Random House, 1984.

Introduction

Sandra Cisneros was born in Chicago in 1954, the daughter of a Mexican father and Chicana mother. Her lyrical vignettes have been classified as both short stories and prose poems. Although she insists her work is not autobiography, she draws upon her childhood experiences growing up among six brothers in a family that moved frequently between the United States and Mexico. In a long interview with Pilar E. Rodriguez Aranda (*Americas Review* 18, no. 1 (Spring 1990): 64-80), Cisneros said, "All fiction is non-fiction. Every piece of fiction is based on something that really happened. On the other hand, it's not autobiography because my family would be the first to confess: 'Well it didn't happen that way.' They always contradict my stories. They don't understand I'm not writing autobiography. What I'm doing is I'm writing true stories. They're all stories I lived, or witnessed, or heard; stories that were told to me. I collected those stories and I arranged them in order so they would be clear and cohesive. Because in real life, there's no order."

Her Latino ethnic heritage, especially the pressure to conform to traditional female roles, informs the conflict of Esperanza Cordero, the narrator of her most popular work, *The House on Mango Street.* As Cisneros points out, "It's very strange to be straddling these two cultures, and to try to define some middle ground so that you don't commit suicide or you don't become so depressed or you don't self-explode.... At the same time, none of us wants to abandon our culture. We're very Mexican, we're all very Chicanas. Part of being Mexicana is that love and that affinity we have for our *cultura.*"

During a class discussion of the French philosopher Gaston Bachelard's house metaphor in *The Poetics of Space* at the University of Iowa's Writers Workshop in the late 1970s, Cisneros realized for the first time that her experiences as an Hispanic woman could become her own unique subject matter. It took five years to fashion *The House on Mango Street,* which narrates and celebrates the conflicts of gender, class, economic condition, age, and cultural loyalty.

Reading 10

"My Name" (pages 10–11)

In English my name means hope. In Spanish it means too many letters. It means sadness, it means waiting. It is like the number nine. A muddy color. It is the Mexican records my father plays on Sunday morning when he is shaving, songs like sobbing.

It is my great-grandmother's name and now it is mine. She was a horse woman too, born like me in the Chinese year of the horse—which is supposed to be bad luck if you're born female—but I think this is a Chinese lie because the Chinese, like the Mexicans, don't like their women strong.

My great-grandmother. I would've liked to have known her, a wild horse of a woman, so wild she wouldn't marry. Until my great-grandfather threw a sack over her head and carried her off. Just like that, as if she were a fancy chandelier. That's the way he did it.

And the story goes she never forgave him. She looked out the window her whole life, the way so many women sit their sadness on an elbow. I wonder if she made the best with what she got or was she sorry because she couldn't be all the things she wanted to be. Esperanza. I have inherited her name, but I don't want to inherit her place by the window.

At school they say my name funny as if the syllables were made out of tin and hurt the roof of your mouth. But in Spanish my name is made out of a softer something, like silver, not quite as thick as sister's name—Magdalena—which is uglier than mine. Magdalena who at least can come home and become Nenny. But I am always Esperanza.

I would like to baptize myself under a new name, a name more like the real me, the one nobody sees. Esperanza as Lisandra or Maritza or Zeze the X. Yes. Something like Zeze the X will do.

Reading 11

"Bums in the Attic" (pages 86–87)

I want a house on a hill like the ones with the gardens where Papa works. We go on Sundays, Papa's day off. I used to go. I don't anymore. You don't like to go out with us, Papa says. Getting too old? Getting too stuck-up, says Nenny. I don't tell them I am ashamed—all of us staring out the window like the hungry. I am tired of looking at what we can't have. When we win the lottery…Mama begins, and then I stop listening.

People who live on hills sleep so close to the stars they forget those of us who live too much on earth. They don't look down at all except to be content to live on hills. They have nothing to do with last week's garbage or fear of rats. Night comes. Nothing wakes them but the wind.

One day I'll own my own house, but I won't forget who I am or where I came from. Passing bums will ask, Can I come in? I'll offer them the attic, ask them to stay, because I know how it is to be without a house.

Some days after dinner, guests and I will sit in front of a fire. Floorboards will squeak upstairs. The attic grumble.

Rats? they'll ask.

Bums, I'll say, and I'll be happy.

Reading 12

"Beautiful and Cruel" (pages 88–89)

I am an ugly daughter. I am the one nobody comes for.

Nenny says she won't wait her whole life for a husband to come and get her, that Minerva's sister left her mother's house by having a baby, but she doesn't want to go that way either. She wants things all her own, to pick and choose. Nenny has pretty eyes and it's easy to talk that way if you are pretty.

My mother says when I get older my dusty hair will settle and my blouse will learn to stay clean, but I have decided not to grow up tame like the others who lay their necks on the threshold waiting for the ball and chain.

In the movies there is always one with red red lips who is beautiful and cruel. She is the one who drives the men crazy and laughs them all away. Her power is her own. She will not give it away.

I have begun my own quiet war. Simple. Sure. I am one who leaves the table like a man, without putting back the chair or picking up the plate.

Reading 13

"Mango Says Goodbye Sometimes" (pages 109-10)

I like to tell stories. I tell them inside my head. I tell them after the mailman says, Here's your mail. Here's your mail he said.

I make a story for my life, for each step my brown shoe takes. I say, "And so she trudged up the wooden stairs, her sad brown shoes taking her to the house she never liked."

I like to tell stories. I am going to tell you a story about a girl who didn't want to belong.

We didn't always live on Mango Street. Before that we lived on Loomis on the third floor, and before that we lived on Keeler. Before Keeler it was Paulina, but what I remember most is Mango Street, sad red house, the house I belong but do not belong to.

I put it down on paper and then the ghost does not ache so much. I write it down and Mango says goodbye sometimes. She does not hold me with both arms. She sets me free.

One day I will pack my bags of books and paper. One day I will say goodbye to Mango. I am too strong for her to keep me here forever. One day I will go away.

Friends and neighbors will say, What happened to that Esperanza? Where did she go with all those books and paper? Why did she march so far away?

They will not know I have gone away to come back. For the ones I left behind. For the ones who cannot out.

Student Handout

The Burakumin of Japan

Among prevailing stereotypic images of Japan is the one declaring a kind of ethnic, racial, and linguistic homogeneity and social harmony among Japanese people. While there is some truth in this image, especially when the social composition of its people is compared with the ethnic, racial, and linguistic diversities of the United States or the former Soviet Union, for instance, the portrait of harmony and consensus, homogeneity and cultural uniformity is overdrawn.

There are significant numbers of minorities in Japan—more than one million Koreans, thousands of other *gaijin* (foreign persons), and large numbers of Iranians and East Asians. By far the biggest minority, with an estimated population of 1,150,000, to 2,000,000, are the Burakumin who have no distinct cultural and physical attributes separating them from other Japanese. Their origins are shrouded in mystery, but most scholars agree that they were an occupational outcaste group who carried out economically important but culturally despised tasks, for example, working with animals and meat, a Buddhist taboo; preparing leather-related weapons of war; carrying on the water trades; handling the dead, and so on. Burakumin are linguistically, culturally, and racially identical to other Japanese. Nonetheless, they are a minority group, occupying a subordinate position, suffering from social disabilities, sharing a common identity, living, not atypically, in nearly 6,452 segregated communities throughout Japan. The totals would be much higher if they included those who have passed into majority neighborhoods in Tokyo and other large cities and hamlets.

The existence of the Burakumin is not advertised widely by the Japanese, who take pride in their egalitarian commitments and who value inclusiveness. The Burakumin symbolize and reveal the existence of discrimination, thus offering a challenge to the Japanese sense of justice and commitment to compassion. The Burakumin have also been the focus of some of the more creative if controversial actions of political groups seeking to right the wrongs of past discrimination. They are a people who have, for the last eight decades, tried to undo the social, political, and economic injustices they have suffered but cannot quite overcome the centuries-old tradition of degraded status that is their legacy.

There are few more inherently tragic situations than the one besetting the children of a low-status minority group in Japan. They live in a so-called group society, but they belong to a group of beings cast out, believed polluted and dirty. For the children of this group, their bonds to their group create the very basis for their individual degradation, presenting them with an excruciating double-bind. To love their families is to hate themselves and to court indignity. On the other hand, to join other groups and assimilate means to forsake those whom they have loved and on whom they have relied—an intolerable condition in a group society.

The Burakumin are generally understood to be descendants of the Eta-Hinin, a kind of untouchable or pariah group which emerged during the Tokugawa Period (1603–1868).

1603-1868: Tokugawa Era

During this period of relative international isolation, the Japanese legalized a code that reinforced and elaborated a rigid hierarchical social structure: aristocrats, peasants, artisans, and merchants. A pariah group, disparagingly called *Eta* (defilement abundant) *Hinin* (nonhuman) people, became separated physically, occupationally, and socially from all other groups. Their status was so low they did not even appear in the Tokugawa social hierarchy.

This special status was announced through social markers and regulations, which required that they

- eat separately
- wear particular clothing and slippers
- avoid ordinary hairstyles
- stay out of households of commoners
- stay in their own hovels at night

Other stereotypes emerged that labeled the Burakumin as violent, dirty, smelly, corrupt, sexually promiscuous, and (like animals) without thumbs. Popular superstitions included beliefs that Burakumin were like reptiles, cold to the touch. Considered to be polluted and defiled, their work was of low economic and social status: animal slaughter, leather work, bamboo craft, peddling, sewage removal, unskilled labor, shoe making, itinerant entertainment, and gardening. Today, some Burakumin groups claim a major role in the creation of Kabuki theater and Japanese landscape gardening.

1868-1912: Meiji Era

Political Organization and Official Policy Changes

During this period, the Tokugawa social structure was reconstituted, a Burakumin emancipation ordinance promulgated, and a policy established "...abolishing the contemptuous names" and renaming the group "new commoners," thus integrating them as a category in a social hierarchy.

1912-1926: Taisho Era

Emergence of an Active Visible Political Presence

This era saw the formation of *Suiheisha*, or Leveller's Association, the first national Burakumin organization committed to civil rights and militant confrontation as a political tactic.

1926-1968: Showa Era

Suiheisha disbanded and was replaced by the National Committee for Burakumin Liberation. Its political methods shifted from those that were exclusively confrontational to those that were more coalitional. In 1955 the National Committee changed its name to *Kaihodomei* or Burakumin Emancipation League, extended its organizational network to include more and more groups, and is today affiliated with the Socialist Party in Japan. By 1964, in the rubble and misery after World War II, the Burakumin suffered even more. For example, in the Junan community in Shikoku, living conditions were shabby and dilapidated, traditional crafts had been destroyed, and employment was limited to low-status, traditionally unsafe, and demeaning labor. Seventy percent received public welfare and only sixty persons worked on government-supported projects. Only three people ran stores. Educationally, their academic performance was low, and their schools were of poor quality. Sanctions against intermarriage persisted, as did employment discrimination practices.

1968-1992: Showa Era

Attempts to Equalize Conditions

In 1968 family registries were officially sealed. These are records of ancestry which were open to the public until 1968, providing information that allowed employers, potential marriage partners, government officials, and others to determine Burakumin ancestry and single out members of the group for discrimination. Although records are now legally hidden from public view, Burakumin activists insist that such information is still available and widely disseminated. In 1969 the Law on Special Measures for Regional Improvement provided government support for the next twelve years for the following social initiatives:

- improving living conditions
- building an industrial infrastructure
- improving child-care facilities
- expanding vocational education
- restructuring the educational system

Increasing High School and College Attendance

In 1982 the Law on Special Measures for Regional Improvement extended support for five more years.

1993-Present: Heisei Era

Despite enormous opposition the Special Measures Law was once again extended but at diminished funding levels. Today, it is said that more than 68 billion yen ($523,000,000) have been distributed to implement this law.

Scholarly Works

Gibson, Margaret A., and John Ogbu. *Minority Status and Schooling: A Comparative Study of Immigrant and Involuntary Minorities.* New York: Garland Press, 1991.

Herbst, Philip H. *The Color of Words: An Encylopædic Dictionary of Ethnic Bias in the United States.* Yarmouth, ME: Intercultural Press, 1997.

Hirasawa, Yasumasa. "The Education of Minority Children in Japan." In *Transcending Stereotypes: Discovering Japanese Culture and Education,* edited by Barbara Finkelstein, Joseph J. Tobin, and Anne E. Imamura. Yarmouth, ME: Intercultural Press, 1991.

Lewis, Tom, and Robert Jungman. *On Being Foreign: Culture Shock in Short Fiction, An International Anthology.* Yarmouth, ME: Intercultural Press, 1986.

Shimahara, Nobuo K. "Toward the Equality of a Japanese Minority: The Case of Burakumin," *Comparative Education Review* 20, no. 3 (1994): 339-53.

3

Seeing through Images: Cultural Learning through Film

Alan Chalk

Introduction: Using International Films to Teach about Culture

Videos, like objects and works of autobiography and autobiographical fiction, are invaluable sources of cultural information and education. Indeed, the power of film to shape what is known and knowable is immense, especially in this day and age when people increasingly rely on television, movies, and electronic forms of communication to acquire cultural knowledge and understanding.

Filmmakers, like novelists and anthropologists, create cultural images, transmit information, reveal cultural habits, and otherwise invite viewers to look in upon a culture and a country. Documentaries and travelogues present cultural montages for audiences as outsiders to observe and absorb. Feature films, on the other hand, are made primarily for cultural insiders. For the intercultural teacher films present an array of insider-outsider perspectives rich in possibilities for cultural education. Through the medium of film, students experience culture vicariously, interacting with peoples and places that would be otherwise inaccessible, exotic, or strange. Through film's evocative power and true-to-life qualities, students are provided with opportunities to revisit the cultural myths that they have learned and that they, often unconsciously, use to make sense of the world, its peoples, and its happenings. At the same time, however, the very cultural myths with which students make sense of their environment can also make non-sense in unfamiliar cultural settings.[1]

Through the exploration of international film as a form of visual world literature, teachers can help students enter into the experience of other cultures, discovering how those who are culturally different express love, fear, joy, and sorrow and cope with life's comedies, tragedies, and dilemmas. These films engage students in the discovery of alternative perspectives and ways of knowing, being,

---

[1] Barbara Finkelstein, "Reflections on Refraction," The Gail Kelly Memorial Lecture (Buffalo, NY: State University of New York, 1995) available from the International Center for the Study of Education Policy and Human Values, University of Maryland, College Park, 20742. See also: Barbara Finkelstein, Sarah Pickert, Tracy Mahoney, and Douglas Barry, *Discovering Culture in Education: An Approach to Cultural Education Program Evaluation* (Washington, DC: ERIC Clearinghouse on Assessment and Evaluation, 1998).

thinking, and doing; the films also reveal patterns of social behavior and organization, exposing culturally unfamiliar habits and making the once exotic more approachable. Carefully studied and sensitively presented, films can also enable both teachers and students to revisit controversial historical events and issues.

In this chapter, we explore the medium of film as a history-making genre, studying how it can shape collective memory, construct and deconstruct images, define insiders and outsiders, and both reflect and create an historical narrative through the imagery used, the stories told, and the portraits of heroes and heroines drawn.

This chapter focuses on the use of the 1970 Japanese and American coproduction *Tora! Tora! Tora!* as an example of binational and intercultural historical narrative, linking the study of film to considerations of historical interpretation, cultural stereotyping, and the importance of point of view. Through the close study of *Tora! Tora! Tora!* students can be challenged to reexamine and reinterpret an historical event from different national and cultural points of view.

Even now, decades after the end of hostilities, the memory of the December 7 attack on Pearl Harbor continues to play a significant part in the prevailing American view of the war and the view of the Japanese as a sneaky, treacherous, inhumane, and duplicitous people. *Tora! Tora! Tora!*, although made primarily for American audiences, presents the attack with remarkable historical accuracy, representing both American and Japanese points of view, revealing the complex prelude to the Pacific War, and putting new faces on previously defined enemies.

Relationships between the two nations have, of course, changed over the last half century. But culturally stereotyped views of the Japanese survive nonetheless. The imagery that endures is not reflected as it was during wartime, in demonized visual images, but more subtly, in the forms of historical storytelling and in interpretations that persist. In many history textbooks, the dominating historical narrative attributes U.S. involvement in the Pacific War solely to the bombing of Pearl Harbor. Japanese aggression constitutes a sufficient explanation of the cause of the war. Little attention is paid to Western colonial involvement in Asia, American expansion into the Pacific, and Japanese geopolitical and socioeconomic concerns.

One of the goals of the lessons that follow is to help students examine this American national narrative, consider the Japanese perspective, and view history as a dynamic, evolving, culturally revealing process with multiple narratives that continue to be revised. As Carol Gluck has put it, history constitutes, among other things, "...stories that nations tell themselves and teach their children in the name less of the past than the present." She calls nationalistic storytelling "mythistory" and suggests that "...the myths are as important as the history and both are continually reworked."[2]

The ritual and fluid power of history is also a theme in the work of Professor Akira Iriye who, in a presidential address to the American Historical Association,

---

2 Carol Gluck, "The Idea of Showa," *Daedalus* (Summer 1990): 1–26.

suggested that it was time to go beyond the nationalistic framework of history and write and teach a binational and international history of war. He suggested, as an example, that Japanese and American teachers approach controversial subjects, such as the attack on Pearl Harbor and the atomic bombings, in ways that open up questions of fact and interpretation.[3]

In effect, both Gluck and Iriye are calling for new critical approaches to the study of history, seeing the role of history teachers as cultural mediators who, as they teach, help students to understand history as involving international and intercultural processes.

The lessons that follow engage students in the study of a specific historic event, the bombing of Pearl Harbor, asking them to consider the roles that the wartime national narrative, propaganda, and cultural perception have played in the shaping of historical understanding. Lesson 1 focuses on the 1942–43 documentary film, *December 7th,* as a primary source of the wartime narrative.

The remaining lessons center on *Tora! Tora! Tora!* and alternative points of view about the origins and causes of war, the moral dilemmas of the decision to go to war, the complexity of cause and effect in history, and the importance of wartime decision makers Admiral Yamamoto, Admiral Kimmel, and General Short.

The chapter includes appendices that provide teachers and students with instructional aids, useful information, and a listing of film and print resources. Taken together, the lessons and appendices provide an instructional chapter that enables teachers and students to discover the role of film in creating and retelling history. It also invites students to experience and empathize with culturally alternative points of view, to engage in a critical and creative dialogue with each other about evolving historical perspectives, and in the process, to begin to discover and understand how stereotypes and perceptions based on national narratives impact history and its retelling.

The use of film as a resource to teach about other cultures requires teachers to help students learn to "read" a film and how to view it critically for historical accuracy. Even though students will have already viewed hundreds if not thousands of films, most will be unable to analyze this medium as a construction of image and sound, to appreciate it as a dramatic and aesthetic medium, or to approach it in search of information and cultural understanding. These lessons will help students learn to decode what they see, reflect on their biases and points of view, suspend judgment, and while doing so, dwell in the experience of others and discover the world with new eyes.[4]

---

[3] Akira Iriye, "Understanding Japan-U.S. Relations, 1945-1995," *Japan Quarterly,* 40, no. 3 (July-September 1995), 256-64.

[4] Barbara Finkelstein, "Dwelling in the Experience of Others: Intercultural Collaboration in Action, Japanese Dimensions," in *Internationalizing the U.S. Classroom: Japan as a Model,* edited by Linda Wojtan and Donald Spence (Bloomington, IN: ERIC Clearinghouse for Social Studies/Social Science Education and the National Clearinghouse for United States-Japan Studies, 1992.

Lesson 1—Wartime Documentaries as Cultural Reflections: U.S. Narratives on Pearl Harbor and the Opening of the Pacific War

Introduction

The purpose of this lesson is to use John Ford's 1942–43 *December 7th* wartime documentary film to examine and question the original U.S. national narrative of the Japanese attack at Pearl Harbor and the opening of the Pacific War. Because this narrative grew out of wartime propaganda and survives in public memory and many U.S. and world history textbooks, a teacher must begin with it and with the related knowledge and attitudes the students bring to the class.

While President Roosevelt's "A date which will live in infamy" speech, delivered to the U.S. Congress on December 8, 1941, laid the foundation of the narrative's "unprovoked sneak attack," Ford's Academy Award-winning documentary transformed this view into visual form and became the archetypal source for all Pearl Harbor and Pacific War documentaries subsequently produced. Ironically, the film's images and sequences have become a part of public memory and documentary history. The problem is that Ford's film contains very little actual footage of the attack; most of the film's action scenes, although based on eyewitness information, the few available photographs, and some film footage, were re-created in Hollywood. One of the most frequently borrowed scenes shows Japanese planes dropping bombs on the U.S. fleet below. These are actually American planes with Japanese insignia. Even *Tora! Tora! Tora!,* while working toward historical authenticity, re-creates many of Ford's attack sequences.

December 7th, as Ford originally produced it, was eighty-two minutes long, a combination of Hollywood style and government propaganda, portraying the Japanese Americans as potential spies and traitors. Even so, the Navy accused the movie of giving the impression that our military forces were not on the job and ordered the negatives confiscated as "damaging to morale." The following year a pared-down, thirty-five minute version of the move was released, winning John Ford an Academy Award.

In 1991, in honor of the fiftieth anniversary of Pearl Harbor, *December 7th* was rereleased, restored in full to its original eighty-two-minute length. This complete version is available at quality video rental stores; the shorter version may be difficult to obtain. Whereas the entire film can be studied as an example of wartime propaganda, this approach focuses on the attack scenes. Students are asked to examine the film closely to try to determine which scenes are authentic and which have been re-created.

This lesson represents the beginning of the students' quest for some understanding of the complex historical foundation of the Japanese attack at Pearl Harbor and the opening of the Pacific War. Further, it establishes the role of stereotypes and perceptions of "the enemy" that contributed to the making of the national war narrative.

It is important for teachers to preview the film at least once in its entirety and to select the passages to be used.

Objective: To have the students, through viewing the film *December 7th,*

- determine—prior to these lessons—their knowledge and attitudes regarding the Pearl Harbor attack and their current feelings about Japan and the Japanese. A student survey is provided in Appendix A: Survey of Student Knowledge and Attitudes.
- establish the basic facts (what happened, where, when) of the historical event, to provide a perspective on the wartime national narrative of the attack, and to ask the key questions which will be used to examine that narrative through this unit.
- generate questions such as: What is historical truth? How is it achieved?
- if the full eighty-two-minute version is shown, to examine the mixed perceptions of Americans toward the Japanese Hawaiians (and by extension, Japanese Americans in general) both prior to and following the attack on Pearl Harbor.
- recognize the power of film to shape the public's wartime and postwar view of the Pearl Harbor attack and to encourage a critical attitude and development of the skills necessary to examine documentaries and film "re-creations" for their truthful or factual depiction of events.

Materials: Survey of Student Knowledge and Attitudes (see Appendix A); Roosevelt's "A date which will live in infamy" speech; John Ford's 1942 documentary on Pearl Harbor, *December 7th,* either the thirty-five minute version or the original eighty-two minute restored version (see Appendix E: Selected Audiovisuals and Print Sources).

Time: Two class periods

Procedure

1. Prior to any discussion of the Pearl Harbor attack, conduct the student information survey. Assure the students it will be used only for class information and for self-evaluation at the end of the unit. Allow students as much time as they need to complete the survey. After collecting it, ask and discuss briefly where the information and views they have may have come from (other courses, family members, TV, films, etc.).
2. Hand out copies of Roosevelt's "Infamy" speech and read aloud paragraph one and the final five paragraphs beginning "Always will we remember...." Ask and discuss what phrases and words would be the most powerful and effective in moving the U.S. Congress to declare and the public to accept a declaration of war against Japan.

3. Show an excerpt of John Ford's *December 7th* (14-16 minutes: the passage with the Japanese planes preparing to attack, through the end of the attack and the mention of FDR's "Infamy" speech. In the thirty-five-minute version this will be minutes 6 to 20; in the eighty-two-minute version this will be minutes 44 to 60.) If time allows, the showing of either film in its entirety can open discussion about wartime racial perceptions of the Japanese and Japanese Americans.
4. Discussion questions:
    a. What are the implications of this film as one of the major sources of the public's memory of Pearl Harbor? Do you think it is a true version of the attack? In what ways yes, and in what ways no?
    b. Considering the film as a propaganda piece, what words, scenes, music, and other Hollywood techniques combined to help shape American attitudes and perceptions of the Japanese, to stir the American people to righteous indignation and the willingness to go to war?
    c. If the entire film is shown, discuss, in conjunction with the pre- and postattack sections of the film, what evidence you found of American ambivalence toward the Japanese Americans of Hawaii.

Assignment

1. Compare the film with the Pearl Harbor coverage found in any available text. In what ways does the text reflect, question, or change the film narrative of an unprovoked, sneak (or surprise) attack? Compare and contrast passages on Pearl Harbor from several texts, old and recent.
2. Have the students study the Time Line of U.S.-Japan Relations, 1841-1941 (see Appendix B), and on a map of the Pacific locate the possessions acquired by the United States and Japan from 1846 through 1941, marking them on the map with different colors for the United States and Japan. Assuming the point of view of either Japan or the United States, write a position paper about the perceptions and conclusions one might draw concerning the expansion of the other nation. Speculate as to the possible motives and goals of the other nation's expansion and how that might affect the other nation's future. How might this conflict of national interests lead to war?

Evaluation: If this lesson is being used alone, evaluation of how well the students have achieved the objectives must depend on the quality of their participation in observing, analyzing, and discussing the visual materials. If further evaluation is necessary at this point, one of the two written assignments above can be used. If all four lessons will be used, evaluation can either be delayed until the end (see Evaluation, page 122) or it can follow each lesson as the teacher deems necessary.

Lesson 2–*Tora! Tora! Tora!* and the Cross-Cultural Perspectives of the Japanese and U.S. Roads to Pearl Harbor

Introduction

The purpose of this lesson is to use *Tora! Tora! Tora!* to examine U.S. and Japanese perspectives of the prelude to and the opening of the war between the two nations. The approach works through two puzzling questions: On the Japanese side, why does Admiral Yamamoto lead Japan into a war he feels his nation cannot in the long run win? On the U.S. side, why is it that with so many obvious warnings, the American military forces in Hawaii are caught off guard?

The film interweaves the Japanese and U.S. narratives in a loose chronology from August 1939 through December 7, 1941, when they converge in the attack at Pearl Harbor. While the film opens with Admiral Yamamoto's taking command of the Japanese Combined Fleet in 1939, the U.S. scenes begin with the negotiations between the United States and Japan in the spring of 1941. Gradually, however, the two narratives move into fairly clear and accurate concurrent rhythm. A time line of the events leading to the attack is provided (see Appendix B: Time Line of U.S.-Japan Relations, 1841-1941).

If the entire film is to be studied, it can be divided into four sections, each around thirty-five minutes long. Showing the sequence in four consecutive class periods covers the entire film and allows a little time in each period for brief discussion and homework assignments. The following class or classes can then be devoted to the selected learning activities.

If the edited approach is chosen, sections one, two, and three dealing with the events leading to the attack can be reduced to one class period by selecting and fast-forwarding between premarked sequences.

The following objectives and procedures offer several choices which work within different time frames and lead to different learning activities.

Objective: To have the students, through viewing the film *Tora! Tora! Tora!*,

- learn how to use film to explore cross-cultural perspectives; here, the Japanese and U.S. perspectives of events leading to the attack at Pearl Harbor and the opening of the war between the two nations.
- study the U.S. scenes and compare the film's Pearl Harbor narrative with the wartime narrative of an unprovoked "sneak" attack and other narratives contained in history and social studies texts.
- study the Japanese scenes as a representation of a Japanese perspective of the opening of the war to determine (1) what, from a Japanese point of view, the causes of or reasons for the war were, (2) what the short- and long-range goals of the attack were, and (3) why, if Admiral Yamamoto (and possibly others) felt that Japan could not defeat the United States in a prolonged war, he planned and executed the attack to initiate the war.

- analyze the film as two distinct national and cultural narratives on the Pearl Harbor attack and the opening of the war and assess separately the tone, attitude, and interpretation of the Japanese (Toshio Masuda and Kinji Fukasaku) and United States (Richard Fleischer) directors.
- evaluate the role and responsibility of Admiral Yamamoto in the Pearl Harbor attack prior to an official declaration of war; and also the responsibilities of Admiral Kimmel and General Short for the Pearl Harbor failure of American defenses.

Materials: The film or video *Tora! Tora! Tora!* If the full film is not being shown, it should be previewed on the VCR to note on the counter where the selected scenes are located.

Time: Three class periods

Procedure

1. Ask the students to think about what might be considered possible causes of the war from both Japanese and U.S. points of view. Before viewing the film, review the time line of sequential events leading to the attack from 1939-41, the period the film covers. (See Appendix B: Time Line of U.S.-Japan Relations, 1841–1941.)
2. Announce that the class will now view and study *Tora! Tora! Tora!*, a 1970 collaborative U.S.-Japan film production re-creating the events leading to and the attack on Pearl Harbor. Note that while most supposedly historical feature films fictionalize for commercial reasons, this film is carefully researched and presented with a high degree of historical accuracy. (For students wishing to verify or deepen their understanding of any of the events or scenes in the film, Gordon Prange's book *At Dawn We Slept* is a primary source.)
3. Divide the class into two groups—one, to analyze the U.S. scenes and story; the other, the Japanese scenes and story. They are, while viewing and later discussing the film, to take notes on the following questions*:

   For both groups:

   a. What differences do you see between *December 7th* and *Tora! Tora! Tora!* in terms of the U.S. national narrative regarding the war?

   b. Do any of the Japanese or Americans think that the war can be avoided? If so, who? As you study the events leading to the war, do you consider the war inevitable or could it have been prevented? Explain.

---

* Additional study questions can be found in Appendix C.

c. Analyze the differences in tone and attitude between the Japanese and American directors in telling their nations' stories. How do music, mood, script, and other film techniques reinforce those differences?

For the Japan group:

a. From a Japanese point of view in 1941, what are the apparent causes or reasons for the war (from both outside and inside Japan)?
b. What are the Japanese short- and long-range goals for the attack on Pearl Harbor?
c. If Admiral Yamamoto felt Japan could not defeat the United States in a prolonged war, why does he finally lead his nation and people into the war?

For the U.S. group:

a. From a U.S. point of view in 1941, what are the apparent causes of the war?
b. What actions or decisions suggest an expectation of war with Japan? Why does the United States expect war?
c. What failures in communication and in defense preparation result in the United States being unprepared for or surprised by the eventual attack?

4. Show the film in three sessions: one is the opening through scene 20 (excluding credits, 34 minutes) covering the causes and preparations for war. At the end of this section Admiral Yamamoto tells his staff that the war now seems unavoidable and that they are committed to the Pearl Harbor gamble. Session two includes scenes 21 through 42 (about 33 minutes) and deals with the above questions. The final scene shows the Japanese task force of six carriers, two battleships, three cruisers, eight destroyers, three oilers, one supply ship, and two submarines (a total of twenty-five ships) having traveled undetected for the 3,400 nautical miles from Japan to north of Hawaii. The attack is about to begin. Session three is the morning of December 7, 1941, scenes 43 through 65 (about 35 minutes), ending with two historic messages. The first is "Tora, Tora, Tora" ("Tiger, Tiger, Tiger"), Commander Fuchida's message that the plan has worked, that the first wave of 185 torpedo planes, bombers, and fighters has reached the target without resistance. The second message is from two U.S. officers to all U.S. forces: "Air raid, Pearl Harbor. This is no drill." The second wave of 170 planes brings the Japanese total to 355 attacking aircraft.

Assignment: The following assignments constitute preparation for some of the various learning activities possible. Here the teacher may focus the class on one activity or assign small-group or individualized activities.

1. The U.S. group: The students should make lists comparing the two films and a class text in relation to presentation and interpretation of the attack. Advanced students should research other texts and scholarly sources (see Appendix E: Selected Audiovisuals and Print Sources).
2. The Japan group: The students should list the apparent causes of and reasons for the war from the Japanese point of view as presented in the film. The U.S. presence in the Pacific from the Japanese point of view can provide other possibilities. Although research into Japanese sources may be difficult, advanced students should seek out these sources in such studies as *Pearl Harbor Re-examined* and other scholarly works. (See also Appendix D.)
3. This assignment recognizes that *Tora! Tora! Tora!* is a film. Although the film tries to be historically objective and accurate, the scriptwriters, actors, and directors cannot help but interpret the historical characters and events. The task here, then, is to view *Tora! Tora! Tora!* as two films—one U.S., the other Japanese—and to compare the work of the directors in presenting and interpreting their Pearl Harbor stories. Students representing their assigned national groups will analyze the tone (relation to audience), attitude (toward the subject), and historical interpretation (perspective and meaning) of their Pearl Harbor stories.

Lesson 3—*Tora! Tora! Tora!*, The Attack: History and Film in Search of Truth

Introduction

The final thirty-six minutes of the film portray a powerful, authentic attack on battleship row and the anchored fleet and on the army and naval airfields with their clusters of parked aircraft. Whereas the scenes are based on Ford's original 1942-43 docudrama *December 7th,* twenty-five years of postwar Pearl Harbor research and improved Hollywood technology have transformed the archetypal images into you-are-there "history." Although libraries offer numerous volumes of print and some actual photographs of the attack and resulting damage, it is *Tora! Tora! Tora!* which may remain the ultimate source of the historical experience.

The last four scenes of the film (about ten minutes) provide ironic closure to the film and connection with retrospective views of the attack. In the first, U.S. Secretary of State Hull is meeting with Japanese Ambassadors Nomura and Kurusu, one hour after the attack on Pearl Harbor. Their message is Japan's ultimatum of its war intention, to be delivered (supposedly) just prior to the attack. Despite the position of the American wartime narrative—that the two ambassadors, along with the Japanese government itself, were guilty of deliberate duplicity throughout the negotiations—the two men do not yet know the attack has taken place. They have been negotiating in good faith. Scholars suggest that both nations were seeking ways to avoid war but were tragically inflexible in their policy goals. Hull's moral outrage (quoted directly from Prange's *At Dawn We Slept*) reflects also the American public's wartime view of Japanese treachery in the "sneak" attack. In the 1941 American war narrative, and to some extent in the continuing view, Japanese treachery at Pearl Harbor ended America's Age of Innocence and forced the nation into World War II. Ironically, in this meeting Hull not only knows about the attack, but he also has had a decoded intercept of the secret Japanese ultimatum since morning.

Further irony is found in the Japanese scenes. In one, Admiral Nagumo confounds his subordinates when he cancels the follow-up raids on Pearl Harbor. In his view they have achieved their goals with minimal losses. He feels it is his duty to return the task force intact to Japan. Because of this decision, the Japanese fail to deal a fatal blow to the facilities and military resources of Pearl Harbor. Prange in *At Dawn We Slept* suggests that in the midst of its greatest victory Japan committed its greatest strategic error of the war. He adds the observation of another Japanese admiral who believed that the decision resulted from the emphasis in the Japanese educational system on knowledge and duty rather than on individual thinking. Note in this scene the faces of the Japanese officers as they momentarily protest Admiral Nagumo's decision, then fall in unquestioningly behind him when the task force begins its return to Japan. Scholars have debated the wisdom and the historical implications of this decision; students might also profit by exploring it.

The final irony is Admiral Yamamoto's concluding remark: "I had intended to deal a fatal blow to the American fleet by attacking Pearl Harbor immediately after Japan's declaration of war. But according to the American radio, Pearl Harbor was attacked fifty-five minutes before the ultimatum was delivered in Washington. I can't imagine anything that would infuriate the Americans more. I fear all we have done is to awaken a sleeping giant and fill him with a terrible resolve." Whether or not Yamamoto actually said this or something like it, the remark is very appropriate if we look back on the outcome of the war. However, this truth was evident that first day when U.S. Secretary of War Stimson wrote in his diary that he was relieved that the indecision was over and that the crisis would unite the American people in a common cause. In retrospect, it was the shock and anger of the American public in response to the news of the attack, "a date which will live in infamy," and the characterization of the Japanese as a treacherous race that overnight unified all Americans and ignited their war effort as a commitment to a "war without mercy against a treacherous foe."

Objective: To have the students, through viewing the last section of *Tora! Tora! Tora!*,

- experience the attack at Pearl Harbor from both Japanese and U.S. viewpoints, seeing it as the basis of each nation's emotional and patriotic response—the Japanese excitement, then awe of victory, the U.S. shock and vulnerability, then anger at defeat.
- understand U.S. Secretary of State Hull's response to Japanese Ambassadors Nomura and Kurusu as a reflection of the moral outrage that fueled the U.S. war effort.
- understand the responses of Japanese Admirals Nagumo and Yamamoto (in contrast to the younger subordinate officers) as a reflection of their (and perhaps others') awareness of the implications of this sudden initial victory and the long war ahead against the United States.
- continue, as in the last lesson, to analyze the film as two distinct national and cultural narratives about one historical event; to understand each director's interpretation of the historical event and its meaning for the present.
- continue, as in the last lesson, to evaluate the role and responsibility of Admiral Yamamoto in the Pearl Harbor attack prior to an official declaration of war.

Materials: The last section of *Tora! Tora! Tora!*

Time: One class period

Procedure

1. Briefly review the previous film section and the assignments.
2. Remind the students that what they are viewing is a re-creation of the attack based on the original 1942 docudrama and the latest historical

research at the time of the 1970 film. Discuss the irony, in this case, of a feature film as the ultimate source of the historical experience.

3. Continue to divide the class into two groups, assigning the responsibility for close study and note taking for the Japanese scenes to one group, the U.S. scenes to the other. Provide the following questions as guides.

   For the U.S. group: Drawing from the introduction to this lesson, ask the students to watch for the scene with U.S. Secretary of State Hull meeting with the Japanese ambassadors who are one hour late in delivering Japan's war ultimatum. Have them study the ambassadors. Are they aware of the attack? Note that Hull not only knows of the attack going on at that moment, but he also has had a copy of the decoded secret Japanese ultimatum since morning. Ask the students to compare and contrast this scene with the description of the same scene in Ford's 1942 Pearl Harbor documentary: "At this very moment, on a quiet Sunday afternoon in Washington, Japan's smooth-talking, grinning envoys Nomura and Kurusu were blandly delivering to Mr. Hull a lengthy protestation of Japan's peace intentions." What are the implications of each film version to these questions: (1) Were the Japanese negotiations merely a screen for planned aggression? (2) Were both the United States and Japan sincere in their efforts to avoid war? (3) Is Hull's moral outrage against the Japanese ultimatum justified? In what ways yes? In what ways no? In what ways does his response reflect the U.S. view of a "sneak" attack and the opening of a "war without mercy against a treacherous foe"?

   For the Japan group: Drawing from the introduction to this lesson, ask the students to study carefully the scenes with Admirals Nagumo and Yamamoto. Note that when Nagumo cancels the follow-up raids on Pearl Harbor, the younger subordinate officers are incredulous, believing they should continue to attack. The admiral believes they have achieved their goals with minimal losses, and his duty is to return the task force intact to Japan. Evaluate his decision.

   Study the response of Admiral Yamamoto to the supposed victory. Although his plan and gamble have resulted in an overwhelming victory, he has reservations. What are they and what is the basis of his concerns?

Assignment: Continuing from lesson 2, this assignment may be directed toward a single learning activity for the entire class or varied small-group or individualized activities. (If the next class is to conclude the unit, the teacher should draw the assignments from lesson 4.)

1. (For the U.S. group) What are the main differences between the American wartime Pearl Harbor narrative, the same coverage in the class history text, and the version of the American story in the film *Tora! Tora! Tora!*?

2. (For the Japan group) What are the main differences between the Japanese Pearl Harbor story in *Tora! Tora! Tora!* and the American wartime narrative?
3. (For both groups) What are the main differences between the Japanese and American perspectives of the Pearl Harbor attack and the war between the two nations?
4. (For both groups) How historically accurate or "true" is the *Tora! Tora! Tora!* version of the events leading to and the attack on Pearl Harbor? How do we know what is historical "truth"?

Lesson 4—Pearl Harbor History: How Film Reflects Multiple Historical Narratives and Conflicting Cultural Perspectives

Introduction

During the fiftieth anniversary commemorations of both the Pearl Harbor attack and, four years later, the atomic bombings of Hiroshima and Nagasaki, a heated debate raged in the U.S. mass media between the defenders of the long-established war narrative and those who would change or rewrite it. The heavy criticism from veterans' organizations and the U.S. Congress, forcing one of the Smithsonian Institution's museums to alter an historical exhibit on the atomic bombings, demonstrated the continuing strength of the old war narrative. In one article, the writer, a veteran of the Pacific War, objected to younger nonveterans attempting to rewrite the history he had lived. Historical revisionism has become a negative term separating generations as well as those who claim historical truth.

The goal in these lessons is to involve the students in the process, the discipline of seeking historical knowledge and truth. Students must learn that history is not an absolute of the past and previous generations, but rather an ongoing, dynamic, evolving process of examining, interpreting, and relating the past to their lives and their world. In recognizing the existence of different national and international historical narratives, they enter into the process of history, taking their first steps toward writing their own narratives.

Objective: To have students (note designation in parentheses for all or specific students)

- effectively use the basic historical facts of the prelude to and attack on Pearl Harbor in a creative, scholarly activity (all).
- demonstrate knowledge of the basic ideas of the original wartime Pearl Harbor narrative and be able to compare them with those found in one or more recent narratives (U.S. group).
- demonstrate cross-cultural knowledge of the basic ideas of the Japanese Pearl Harbor narrative presented in *Tora! Tora! Tora!* and compare them with the American narratives, both the original wartime version and the one used in *Tora! Tora! Tora!* (Japan group).
- use the film and outside readings to suggest and analyze several possible causes of the war between Japan and the United States, some from each nation's point of view (all).
- evaluate the roles and responsibilities of Admiral Yamamoto in the Pearl Harbor attack prior to an official declaration of war, and of Admiral Kimmel and General Short for the failure of U.S. defenses to detect and repulse the Japanese attack.

Materials: Outside scholarly materials and readings may be drawn from the bibliography (see Appendix E).

Time: One to three class periods, depending on necessary planning and presentation time

Procedure

1. Review the homework assignments and encourage reactions to and questions concerning *Tora! Tora! Tora!* and the problem of historical truth in the Pearl Harbor attack and the opening of the war.
2. Use the list of activities below to assign projects or allow students to design their own.
3. After the completion of the unit, the students may be given the opportunity to see and retake the introductory survey and then to discuss and evaluate what they have learned from the unit.

Assignment (large and small group)

1. With the class divided into two groups—one representing the United States, the other, Japan—ask each group to compile a list of all the possible causes of or reasons for their nation going to war. Once the list is completed, they should compare their lists with the list of possible causes in Appendix D. Then each student is to select one cause that led his or her nation to war and write a three- to five-minute speech explaining that position to an audience made up of people from the other country. Before collecting these papers, the teacher may ask several students to read their speeches to the class.
2. Follow the same procedure as for activity number one but tell the students their audience will be Pacific War veterans from the opposing side.
3. During the war the phrase "Remember Pearl Harbor" became a motto and battle cry urging Americans to greater war effort and demanding vengeance against the Japanese for the attack on Pearl Harbor. Although the phrase is occasionally revived in commemorations on the anniversary of the attack, the meaning has changed over the years. Current use suggests keeping America militarily strong and always on guard against a sudden attack by an enemy. It also reminds Americans of how conflicting national policies as well as cultural and racial differences can lead two nations, two peoples, to war. In this view Pearl Harbor represents a turning point for the United States when the nation moved from a position of isolation to one of world leadership. Should we continue to "Remember Pearl Harbor," to reflect on its historical lessons for the present? Or should we allow it to slip quietly back into history where it will no longer stir up war memories along with prejudice and conflict between Americans and Japanese?

With the class divided into U.S. and Japan groups, subdivide each country group into small groups of three or four students. Each small group will work on an editorial of about five hundred words for an international English language newspaper to be distributed in the United States and Japan on December 7. The title and topic will answer the above questions and reflect on the implications of the history of Pearl Harbor on current U.S.-Japan relations.

Assignment (small group or individuals)

1. Write two entries in a journal of a Japanese pilot in the Pearl Harbor attack force—a man who, like Admiral Yamamoto, has mixed feelings about the attack and the coming war against the United States. One entry should be written before and another just after the attack. You may choose Commander Fuchida as your model.
2. Write two entries in a journal of an American naval officer in the Pearl Harbor fleet—a man who has had embassy duty in Tokyo and therefore has some knowledge about Japan and the Japanese. He, too, has mixed feelings about the coming war against Japan. Again, write one entry before and another after the attack.
3. Write an exchange of letters between two former college friends, one Japanese, the other American, written just after the Pearl Harbor attack. Each is now facing the coming war and prospects of having to fight against the other. Even though the nations were then at war, some correspondence did get through via embassy mail and exchanges of citizens.
4. Write an exchange of letters between two high school students (pen pals), one Japanese, the other American, shortly after the fiftieth anniversary of the Pearl Harbor attack. As the new generation, what would they say to one another concerning Pearl Harbor, the war, and current U.S.-Japan relations?
5. Write a letter to the editor for publication in a U.S. newspaper on the anniversary of Pearl Harbor. In it explore Admiral Yamamoto's dilemma. Why, in your opinion, did he feel that Japan had no choice but to attack the United States fleet at Pearl Harbor? Try to explain his thinking about Japan's situation in 1941.
6. Write a letter to the editor titled "Remembering and Forgetting Pearl Harbor." Should your generation in both Japan and the United States "remember" or "forget" Pearl Harbor and the Japanese-American War?
7. Write a film review of *Tora! Tora! Tora!* as an American and Japanese coproduction. Discuss the achievement of the film. Consider the relationship between history and fiction (or art), the use of film in education, and film as an international language.

Evaluation: Evaluation of the lessons in this chapter is difficult because the purpose is the development of student personal involvement in the process of history, and much of the work is done in groups rather than by individuals. You may want to consider two separate grades: one for class involvement, participation, and motivation, and the other for a final group or individual writing project as chosen from the above. It is important to evaluate critical thinking skills as well as the ability to pull information from the film (and if assigned, outside research).

Appendix A

Survey of Student Knowledge and Attitudes

Name:

Grade:

Date:

Please answer only those questions that you can; do not guess. The purpose of this survey is for you to compare your knowledge and attitudes at the beginning and at the end of the unit, at which time your instructor will ask you to fill out the survey a second time.

Background Information

1. Have you studied about Pearl Harbor previously in school?
   yes ___ no ___
   If yes, what course(s)? For how long (approximate number of classes)?

2. Have you read about Pearl Harbor on your own?
   yes ___ no ___
   If yes, please indicate whether the sources were books, magazine articles, or newspapers. Give titles if you remember any.

3. Have you learned about Pearl Harbor from television or movies?
   yes ___ no ___

4. Have you heard or learned about Pearl Harbor from other people?
   yes ___ no ___
   If so, who?

Your Opinions

5. What word do you think the public usually associates with the attack?
   sneak ____ surprise ____ unexpected ____ no idea ____

6. How would you characterize the attack?
   sneak ____ surprise ____ unexpected ____ other ____

7. Were the U.S. government and military expecting war with Japan?
   yes ____ no ____ possibly ____ no idea ____

8. Do you remember the date and time of the attack?
   yes ____ no ____
   If yes, list the day, month, year, and time.

9. Do you feel that the attack was in any way provoked by the United States?
   yes ___ no ___ somewhat ___
   If yes or somewhat, can you suggest in what ways?

10. What was the immediate purpose of the attack?

11. What did the attack accomplish?

12. What were the long-range goals of the war for Japan?

13. What were the main causes of the war between Japan and the United States?

14. What feelings and thoughts do you associate with the phrase "Remember Pearl Harbor"? Do you think we should remember or forget Pearl Harbor? Please explain your answer.

Current Feelings about Japan

15. How do you feel about Japan today?

    ___ basically an unfriendly power and an economic threat

    ___ basically a friendly power but an economic threat

    ___ a friendly power but an economic rival

    ___ a friendly power with an economy interdependent with the United States.

    ___ no thoughts or feelings on the topic

16. How would you characterize your feelings about the Japanese people?

    ___ don't like them; don't trust them

    ___ respect them for what they've accomplished, but don't trust them

    ___ respect them for what they've accomplished; would like to know more about them

    ___ admire them for their accomplishments; like them and their culture

    ___ no feelings on the topic

    ___ other feelings (specify)

Appendix B

Time Line of U.S.-Japan Relations, 1841-1941

U.S. and the West	Japan
1840-42: Opium War; China vs. Great Britain; China defeated, opens five ports, Hong Kong ceded to Britain	1840: Near end of Tokugawa Reign (1603-1868); Japan virtually isolated from world for over 200 years
1845: Texas annexed by U.S.	
1846: Oregon territory acquired from Great Britain	1846: Japan refuses U.S. request for opening of trade relations
1846-48: Mexican-American War, U.S. acquires California and becomes a Pacific power	
1853-54: Commodore Perry and squadron of U.S. steam-powered iron warships arrive in Japan; Perry demands opening of ports to trade	1854: Japan forced to agree to "unequal treaties" and to open ports to U.S. and Western powers
1857-58: U.S. acquires Howland, Baker, Johnston, and Kingman Islands in mid-Pacific	
1867: U.S. buys Alaska and Aleutians	1868: Emperor Meiji ascends throne; Meiji Restoration and Japan's Westernization begin
1869: Opening of Suez Canal	
	1875: Japan acquires Kuril Islands
	1879: Japan acquires Ryukyu Islands (includes Okinawa)
1893-98: U.S. annexes Hawaiian Islands	1894-95: China-Japan War; Japan acquires Formosa (Taiwan), Pescadores Islands, and Liaotung Peninsula; Russia, France, and Germany force Japan to return Liaotung

U.S. and the West	Japan
1898: Spanish-American War; U.S. acquires Puerto Rico, Guam, and the Philippines	
1899: U.S. acquires American Samoa and Wake Island	
	1900: Japanese troops join Western powers in putting down Boxer Rebellion in China
	1904-05: Russian-Japanese War; Japan acquires southern Sakhalin, rights to develop Liaotung Peninsula, and interest in Korea
	1910: Japan annexes Korea
	1912: Death of Emperor Meiji; Emperor Taisho takes throne
1914: Outbreak of World War I; opening of Panama Canal	1914: Japan joins Western allies; declares war on Germany, occupies German Tsingtao in China and islands in the Pacific: Northern Mariana, Caroline, and Marshall
	1915: Japan presents China with twenty-one demands, China accepts sixteen
1917: Russian Revolution; U.S. enters World War I	
1918: End of World War I	1918: U.S. asks Japan to send troops to Siberia
1919: Paris Peace Conference, Treaty of Versailles	1919: Japan participates in peace conference but fails to fully achieve aims
1920: Formation of League of Nations; U.S. refuses to join	1920: Japan becomes a member of the League of Nations; Nikolaevsk incident; Japanese citizens in Siberia massacred
1921-22: Washington Disarmament Conference; ten-year treaty (U.S., Great Britain, Japan, France) to respect each other's Pacific possessions; also a treaty to limit navies (fifteen years) and to respect China	1921-22: Japan finally recognized and respected by U.S. and Western powers but still suspected

U.S. and the West	Japan
1924: U.S. passes Oriental Exclusion Act, an immigration act aimed at preventing Japanese immigrants entry into the U.S.	
	1926: Taisho Emperor dies; Hirohito takes throne; Showa era begins
1929: U.S. stock market crashes, sets off worldwide depression	
1930: London disarmament conference	1930: Military feels betrayed by government concessions in London conference
	1931-32: Manchurian incident, arranged takeover by Japanese military, becomes puppet state, Manchukuo
1932-33: U.S. refuses to recognize Manchuko; League of Nations criticizes Japan's involvement in Manchuria/ Manchukuo	1933: Japan takes over Jehol province; Japan withdraws from League
	1934: Japan breaks from Washington Disarmament Treaty
	1936: Rebellion of young officers, assassinations of government officials; rebellion put down, but military emerges stronger
1937: *U.S.S. Panay* sunk by Japanese planes in China; Japan apologizes	1937: China incident, invasion of China, "Rape" of Nanking
1938: U.S. begins moral embargo of airplanes and parts for Japan; U.S. aid to China; end of Japanese credit	1938: China quagmire; Japan declares "New Order" in Asia
1939: (July) U.S. abrogation of Treaty of Commerce with Japan (Sept.) Germany invades Poland; World War II begins; Russia invades Poland from East; Britain and France declare war on Germany	1939: (Aug.) Admiral Yamamoto appointed Commander-in-Chief of Combined Fleet; Japan sends troops to occupy North Indochina; announces idea of Greater East Asia Co-Prosperity Sphere (Sept.) Tripartite Pact between Japan, Germany, and Italy (Dec.) Admiral Nomura sent to U.S. for peace talks

U.S. and the West	**Japan**
1940: Germany defeats and occupies Denmark, Norway, Holland, Belgium, and France; Battle of Britain begins (Spring) U.S. moves Pacific fleet from California to Pearl Harbor (Nov.) British torpedo planes sink Italian battleships in harbor (Dec.) U.S. embargo on scrap iron and war material for Japan	
1941: (Feb.-Mar.) Rear Admiral Bellinger and Major General Martin (Air Force) file report predicting exact details of Pearl Harbor raid (April) Hull note outlines principles for peace (Aug.) U.S. rejects summit proposal; FDR approves plans for American pilots and ground crews to fly for China ("Flying Tigers") (Sept. 27) U.S. counters Japan's Indochina occupation; freezes Japan's assets in U.S.; stops oil shipments (80 percent of Japan's oil) (Nov. 26) Hull note to Japan demanding withdrawal from Indochina, China, and Manchuria (Nov. 27) War warning message sent to all bases (Dec. 4) U.S. intercepts East Wind Rain message indicating Japan's intent for war with U.S. (Dec. 6) President Roosevelt proposes meeting with Japanese emperor (Dec. 7, 6:30 A.M.) *U.S.S. Ward* sinks Japanese sub outside Pearl Harbor; 7:00 A.M. radar picks up a large number of planes approaching from the north	1941: (Jan.) Peace talks begin in Washington; Japan-U.S.S.R. neutrality pact; Admiral Yamamoto begins Pearl Harbor attack planning (Aug.) Prime Minister Konoye requests summit meeting with FDR in Pacific; Admiral Yamamoto tells prime minister he can hold off U.S. navy for a year at most; Nomura and Kurusu continue negotiations not knowing of planned attack (Sept. 26) Japanese forces occupy southern Indochina (Oct.) General Tojo becomes prime minister (Nov. 26) Task Force sails for Pearl Harbor (Dec. 2) "Climb Mt. Niitaka" order; attack on schedule (Dec. 7, 7:50 A.M.) Tora! Tora! Tora!
(Dec. 7, 8:00 A.M.) Japanese attack Pearl Harbor; Japanese-American War begins	(Dec. 7, 8:00 A.M.) Japanese attack Pearl Harbor; Japanese-American War begins

Appendix C

Additional Study Questions

Study Questions for the Japan Group

First film session (34 minutes)

1. What kind of man is Admiral Yamamoto? What is his position on the impending war? List four adjectives you would use to describe him.
2. Why is Yamamoto so upset by Japan's signing of the Axis Tripartite Pact with Germany? Why do you suppose some of the Japanese leadership wanted that connection with Germany?
3. Why are many of the Japanese depicted here eager to go to war with the United States?
4. Why does Yamamoto conclude that there is little hope for peace and that war plans must go forward?

Second film session (33 minutes)

5. The prime minister quotes a poem by the Emperor: "If all men are brethren, then why are the wind and waves so restless?" What does this poem suggest about the Emperor's view of the impending war?
6. In the same scene Yamamoto says, "We can raise havoc with them for a year. After that I can guarantee nothing." What does this suggest about Yamamoto's view of Japan's chances for victory in the war?
7. What is the role of the Japanese ambassador negotiating in Washington? Is he negotiating in good faith? Or is he a screen for Japan's war intention?

Third film session (35 minutes)

8. In Tokyo General Tojo, the new prime minister, blocks the American president's last-minute message to the Japanese Emperor. Explain why.
9. Yamamoto is concerned that Japan's war ultimatum be delivered on time, at 1:00 p.m., thirty minutes before the attack. Why was this considered to be important?
10. What are the reactions of Genda, Nagumo, and Yamamoto to Fuchida's *Tora! Tora! Tora!*? What do you imagine were the inner thoughts of each man?

Study Questions for the U.S. Group

First film session (34 minutes)

1. What do the military officers in Hawaii fear the most and why?
2. As an American citizen looking back on history, what are your feelings as you watch the strategies being developed and decisions being made by the U.S. military?

Second film session (33 minutes)

3. What is the "magic intercept"?
4. Why do the officers at Pearl Harbor have reason to be confused by the messages they received from Washington?
5. What kind of mood is portrayed in Washington, D.C. and in Hawaii on Saturday night, December 6? How can this be explained?
6. Do you think Admiral Kimmel and General Short are at fault in allowing the U.S. forces to be surprised by the Japanese attack force?

Third film session (35 minutes)

7. Both in this session and earlier, what are the general reactions and expectations of the Americans to the new radar device?
8. How can one explain the fact that General Marshall is out riding his horse on Sunday morning during such a tense time? Is he expecting a Japanese attack somewhere in the Pacific?
9. Why do you think Admiral Stark hesitates to inform Admiral Kimmel in Hawaii of the imminent Japanese attack?
10. In the last hours before the attack, what three errors are committed by the Americans that defy reason? How can they have occurred?

Appendix D

A List of the Responses of U.S. and Japanese Teachers to the Question: What Caused the War between Japan and the United States?

U.S. Perspectives	Japanese Perspectives
Unprovoked "sneak" attack at Pearl Harbor and throughout the Pacific by Japan.	Forced into war by the ABCD (American, British, Chinese, Dutch) encirclement and by American embargoes 1938-1941.
Japan's war of aggression against China and Asia; also atrocities committed 1937-1941.	U.S. economic and military support for China ("Flying Tigers") in its war against Japan.
Japanese colonialism in Asia 1894-1941; wars with China and Russia, taking of Korea and Manchuria, and invasions of China and Southeast Asia.	Over a century of Western colonialism in Asia by England, France, Holland, Germany, and the United States, dominating and enslaving Asians; war of liberation.
Axis Tripartite Pact between Japan, Germany, and Italy aligning Japan with European fascism and aggression.	Axis Tripartite Pact as an anticommunist, anti-Russia move, misinterpreted by the West as identifying Japan with fascism.
Racism—a self-critical view that the West, including Americans, waged a racist campaign against the Japanese and Asians from early in the century so that, at root, the war was racially motivated.	Racism—that the West, including the United States, was racist in its domination and treatment of Asians; that Japan as the leader could free Asia from Western control. (Also self-critical in that Japan waged a racist war in China and throughout Asia.)
Failure of negotiations: Japan inflexible, refusing to stop aggression and to pull out of China and all occupied territories.	Failure of negotiations: U.S. insensitive to Japan's need for resources and land to survive economically; also the 1929 U.S. stock market crash, resulting in worldwide depression and severe economic problems in Japan.

U.S. Perspectives	Japanese Perspectives
Japan's military buildup, ignoring particularly the naval limitation treaties of 1922.	United States military buildup in Roosevelt's six-billion-dollar plan and the move of the Pacific fleet to Pearl Harbor.
Japan's violation of the U.S. "Open Door" economic policy forced on Asia from 1900-present; U.S. and West wanted free access to Asian resources and markets.	The Greater East Asia Co-Prosperity Sphere, a war to liberate and unite Asia under Japanese leadership.
Japanese threats to U.S. resources: rubber, tin, etc. from Southeast Asia and Dutch East Indies.	Oil: September 1941, U.S. embargo, cutting off 80 percent of Japan's oil needs and forcing it to seek oil in Southeast Asia.
Misperception and misunderstanding of Japan's needs, motives, intentions, policies, power. Postwar self-criticism.	Misperception and misunderstanding of U.S. motives, intentions, policies, power. Postwar self-criticism.

Appendix E

Selected Audiovisuals and Print Sources

Required Sources

Attack and Reprisal, videocassette, 55 minutes, black and white, MPI Home Video, Oak Forest, IL.

The Pearl Harbor segment of this video is the 1942 Defense and Navy Departments' "Documentary on the Pearl Harbor Attack." This is a thirty-five-minute edited version of John Ford's original eighty-two-minute film.

December 7th: The Movie, videocassette, 82 minutes, black and white, 1942/1990.

Banned for nearly fifty years, this John Ford version of the Pearl Harbor attack was confiscated by navy officials shortly after its completion in 1942 and was released then only in the thirty-five-minute edited version (see above).

Tora! Tora! Tora!, videocassette, 143 minutes, color, 20th Century Fox, 1970.

This film, a U.S.-Japan coproduction, presents the background events leading to the Pearl Harbor attack. Based closely on Gordon Prange's *At Dawn We Slept*, it is an excellent historical re-creation from both the U.S. and Japanese points of view.

Additional Sources*

American Experience: Pearl Harbor.

Production of American Studies Film Center, WGBH Educational Foundation, and WNET/13, 1991, 90 minutes.

Pearl Harbor: 50 Years After, CNN TV.

Bob Cain host; Asahi cooperation; interviews with Pearl Harbor survivors; study of reasons for surprise and impact on U.S., 74 minutes.

---

* The documentaries made during the war and in the decade following reflect the national and racial biases of that time. As the years pass, moving beyond the fiftieth anniversary, the documentaries achieve greater balance and objectivity.

Pearl Harbor: Two Hours That Changed the World, ABC TV, MPI Home Video.

U.S.-Japan joint production written and anchored by David Brinkley; wide coverage from pre-Pearl Harbor to Hiroshima to present; interviews with U.S. and Japanese survivors of attack and war; scholars with President Bush and Prime Minister Miyazawa; best of the fiftieth-anniversary documentaries, 1 hour and 45 minutes.

Remember Pearl Harbor, CBS TV.

Charles Kuralt and General H. Norman Schwarzkopf present historical footage, photographs, and eyewitness accounts of the attack, 2 hours.

Remembering Pearl Harbor and the U.S.S. Arizona *Memorial.*

Documentary souvenir from Pearl Harbor; narrated by Telly Savalas, 1970s-80s.

World at War Series, Thorn EMI Video, New York.

Volume 6—"Bonzai—Japan Strikes December 1941"; Pearl Harbor and the early victories, 52 minutes.

World War II, CBS Library.

"The Pacific War"; Walter Cronkite, 1961-70s; "The Man Who Spied on Pearl Harbor."

Selected Bibliography

The Road to Pearl Harbor

Agawa, Hiroyuki. *The Reluctant Admiral, Yamamoto and the Imperial Navy.* Rev. ed. Tokyo: Kodansha, 1990.

Barnhart, Michael. *Japan Prepares for Total War: The Search for Economic Security, 1919-1941.* New York: Cornell University Press, 1987.

Dower, John. *War without Mercy: Race and Power in the Pacific War.* New York: Pantheon, 1986.

Ienaga, Saburo. *The Pacific War, 1931-1945.* Rev. ed. New York: Pantheon, 1978.

Iriye, Akira. *Power and Culture: The Japanese American War, 1941-1945.* Cambridge: Harvard University Press, 1981.

Toland, John. *Rising Sun: The Decline and Fall of the Japanese Empire, 1936-1945.* New York: Random House, 1970.

Wray, Harry, and Hilary Conroy, eds. *Japan Examined: Perspectives on Modern Japanese History.* Honolulu: University of Hawaii Press, 1983.

———. *Pearl Harbor Re-examined: Prologue to the Pacific War.* Honolulu: University of Hawaii Press, 1990.

The Pearl Harbor Attack

Prange, Gordon, W. in collaboration with Donald M. Goldstein and Katherine V. Dillon. *At Dawn We Slept: The Untold Story of Pearl Harbor.* New York: McGraw-Hill, 1981.

———. *Pearl Harbor: The Verdict of History.* New York: McGraw-Hill, 1986.

———. *December 7, 1941: The Day the Japanese Attacked Pearl Harbor.* New York: McGraw-Hill, 1988.

———. *God's Samurai: Lead Pilot at Pearl Harbor.* New York: McGraw-Hill, n.d.

Toland, John. *But Not in Shame: The Six Months after Pearl Harbor.* New York: Random House, 1961.

———. *Infamy: Pearl Harbor and Its Aftermath.* New York: Doubleday, 1982.

4

Seeing through Language: Preparing Second or Foreign Language Learners to Explore Culture

Corinne Mantle-Bromley

Introduction

Students enter the second or foreign language classroom with preconceived ideas about the language, its speakers, and the value of language and culture study. While some students eagerly anticipate learning about other peoples and their languages, others do not.

Research confirms the common-sense notion that students' attitudes affect their motivation to learn. This is especially true in the language classroom, where students must take on some of the behaviors (e.g., pronunciation) of the studied cultural group. In fact, students with positive attitudes are more likely to participate in class, continue their language study, and retain more of their language skills over time.[1] Likewise, if students are expected to learn intercultural communication skills in social studies classrooms, their attitudes and beliefs will affect their willingness to accept other ways of behaving and viewing the world as valid alternatives to their own.

A troublesome finding of some studies is that students' attitudes toward the studied language and cultures become less favorable after language study (Gardner 1985; Mantle-Bromley and Miller 1991; Mantle-Bromley 1995). This may be due in part to their unrealistic beliefs about the language learning process. It is not uncommon, for example, for novice second or foreign language learners to believe that they will learn to speak another language very well in less than one year (Mantle-Bromley 1994). This attitudinal slide may also be a result of increased attention to the studied cultural group. Students may resist acceptance of the culture because of ethnocentric blocks and/or preexisting attitudes or beliefs. Students are not usually prepared for the difficulties and frustrations they may encounter in language and culture learning.

Teachers of Japanese language and culture, for example, may find themselves in a unique, paradoxical situation where students simultaneously see Japanese achievements as both admirable and threatening. Many Americans know that

[1] For a review of this research see Robert C. Gardner, *Social Psychology and Second Language Learning: The Role of Attitudes and Motivation* (London: Arnold, 1985).

Japanese students historically score higher on math and science achievement tests than Americans do and that Japanese worker productivity has been higher than that of U.S. workers. Americans also know that the Japanese have dramatically increased their investments in American businesses. While each of these achievements is admirable, U.S. students may see the Japanese as threatening a perceived U.S. economic superiority. It is possible and highly likely that some students will enter the Japanese language class holding suspicious or negative attitudes toward Japanese people. In another case, teachers of Spanish and the diverse cultures of the Spanish-speaking world may find students who believe that Mexican migrant workers (and the lower social status that accompanies their work) are representative of all Spanish speakers. Students' attitudes toward the language and its cultures will reflect their community's attitudes, which may be disparaging or patronizing.

The following lessons were written to help teachers of language and culture begin to address their American students' possibly slanted or one-sided cultural attitudes and beliefs. They were designed with the junior high or middle school program in mind and contain examples from several languages and cultures. The main lessons should take approximately fifty minutes to complete. While the lessons are suitable for more advanced levels and multiple languages and cultures, some adaptation may be needed. Mantle-Bromley (1995) reports that the successful use of these lessons positively influences students' language- and culture-related attitudes.

Background

Three major assumptions provide the theoretical framework for this curriculum. First is the research-based belief that intercultural understanding, the ultimate long-term goal of language and culture study, is developmental (Bennett 1993; Hanvey 1975; Wurzel 1988). While various developmental models exist, authors generally agree that we work through progressive stages as we become more skilled at intercultural understanding. Before students can successfully adapt to a new culture, they will pass through earlier stages of ethnocentrism, confusion, and frustration. Lessons such as the following can help students learn to talk about these aspects of the culture-learning process, thus increasing their skills.

The second assumption, also a component of many developmental intercultural models, is the understanding that the ability to understand others' cultures hinges on a clear conception of one's own (Bennett 1993; Wurzel 1988). Students of culture must recognize that their own perceptions of reality have been constructed within a cultural framework. These lessons challenge students to examine their own culture as an entry to understanding another.

The third assumption of these lessons follows naturally from the first two: If the goals and objectives of this curriculum are to be achieved, they must be constantly revisited and reintegrated into the larger curriculum. Students will vary in their understanding of concepts and in their readiness to progress. The teacher can use these lessons to provide students with both shared experiences and a common vocabulary with which to reexamine cultural issues as the opportunity and/or need arises, increasing the level of sophistication as students' understanding of concepts develops.

The lessons are based on attitude-change theory (Triandis 1971) and culture-learning stages (Bennett 1993; Hanvey 1975; Wurzel 1988), and they have been influenced by many additional authors in the field of intercultural communication.

Goals

It is hoped that through implementation of these lessons, students will

1. strengthen personal reasons for studying other languages and cultures,
2. understand the value of knowing a foreign or second language and understanding its culture(s),
3. broaden awareness of U.S. culture in its many forms,
4. increase awareness of their own attitudes and beliefs, and
5. improve their cross-cultural communication skills.

Underlying premises of these goals are the assumptions that

1. cross-cultural understanding and communication are desirable,
2. students will learn more effectively about others if they first learn about themselves, and
3. culture learning, to be meaningful, must be nonjudgmental.

Evaluation of these overall goals must be an ongoing, formative process that takes into account each student's individual progress. For example, even upper elementary students can, with additional guidance, make "cultural understanding" portfolios from the following lessons, where they demonstrate their own progress toward the five goals. Each lesson additionally has its own objectives which are evaluated within the context of the lesson.

Procedure

When should the lessons be taught? The lessons are designed to be integrated into a beginning-level language or culture class. Ideally, the topic of each lesson will be the cultural focus for one or two weeks, then be integrated into a broader context. The main lesson will take one complete class period; some lessons have short follow-up activities which should be completed within one week of the main lesson.

Won't the lessons take away valuable language learning time? Students will ultimately be more successful in developing second language communication skills if they have an understanding of culture. Furthermore, they will persist in their studies longer if their attitude toward the language and related culture(s) is positive. Because students bring with them potentially harmful attitudes and beliefs, it is critical that teachers help their students work through these blocks to language and culture learning (Mantle-Bromley 1992).

How can I make the learning environment conducive to attitude and culture exploration? The learning environment is a critical factor in any program whose aim is maintaining and/or improving attitudes. The following guidelines are recommended:

1. Accept students' attitudes and help them to explore where they originated. If negative attitudes are ignored or denied, they may never be examined critically and changed.
2. Encourage exploration of all cultural values, beliefs, and traditions. Students' attitudes toward specific cultures will improve as they begin to value cultural diversity in general.
3. Show your students the value you place on the lessons' goals and objectives by implementing the lessons in an important time slot. If the lessons are saved for Friday "easy activities," the students will sense the low priority you place on them. Continue to show the relevance of the lessons and activities after the lessons are completed, and discuss the learning that has taken place.

Note: Materials for each lesson are labeled by the lesson (L1 = Lesson 1) and by the order of appearance within the lesson (H1 = Handout 1). Thus, L1, H1 designates the first handout to be used in Lesson 1. Background readings for the teacher are labeled with an *R*, and those materials that must be prepared by the teacher beforehand (transparency, visual, etc.) are labeled with an *M*.

Lesson 1—Why Learn a Foreign Language/Culture?

Introduction

Many students at the beginning level see little or no value to foreign language and culture study other than facilitating travel or fulfilling a requirement. Students generally begin language study because someone (a parent, a counselor, etc.) has recommended that they do so. Few students have thought about why they might want to learn a foreign language, only that it is one more step toward high school graduation. If these beginning students can develop a more global awareness of reasons to learn other languages and cultures, and if each can determine a personal reason, their motivation to learn may increase.

Objective: By the end of the lesson students will be able to

- describe the importance of second language and culture skills in terms of the economy, the environment, and world peace
- describe the range of jobs connected with the economy, the environment, and world peace for which knowledge of a foreign language and culture would make one especially qualified
- explain what the concept of interdependency means
- explain why language and culture study are necessary in a globally interdependent world
- identify a personal reason for studying other languages and cultures

Materials

- Student handout (L1, H1), located on page 146
- Visuals of global environmental issues, exported products, intercultural conflicts

Time: One full class period and two shorter segments the following week

Procedure

Part 1: Introduction

1. Ask students to brainstorm answers for the following question: Why is it important to learn a foreign language and its culture(s)? Write students' responses on the board.

   Tell the students that the purpose of today's lesson is to try to determine if second or foreign language and culture learning is a luxury or a necessity. Have students look at the board and examine their responses to the question they just answered. Have them determine if they gave reasons that could be considered luxuries (travel, etc.) or if they gave reasons that could be considered necessities (success in business, solution to world problems, etc.).
2. Tell students the "Karima" story, by memory if possible.

Karima

Karima is a sixteen-year-old girl from a royal family in a faraway country. She has been assigned by her father, the king, to learn how it feels to be a teenager in the United States. She should learn what makes teens "tick": what they like and dislike, and also why they do what they do. Before she can return to her own country, she must understand *the American teen.*

Karima, who speaks no English, comes to the United States with Mr. Natadjaja. Mr. Natadjaja is a thirty-five-year-old government official who will be Karima's translator. He speaks both Karima's language and English very well.

Lead students to the realization that without learning the language, Karima's chances of truly understanding American teens will be slim by asking the following questions:

- How should Karima learn about the American teenager?
- What can Karima do to speed up the process?
- How can she best learn how it *feels* to be an American teenager?

Part 2: Reasons to Learn a Foreign Language (Environment, Economy, World Peace)

1. Show students visuals of environmental problems or catastrophes. See the magazine selections below for possible visuals regarding acid rain, destruction of rain forest, endangered species, nuclear disasters, and so on.

   Jon R. Luoma, "Acid Murder No Longer a Mystery," *Audubon* (November 1988): 126-35.
   "What Japan Thinks of Us," *Newsweek* (2 April 1990), 18-22.
   Robert Repetto, "Deforestation in the Tropics," *Scientific American* (April 1990): 36-42.
   "High Tech Anxiety," *U.S. News & World Report* (19 May 1986), 20-21.
   "Yes, We Mind If They Smoke," *U.S. News & World Report* (25 July 1988), 43-45.

   Go through the following sequence for each visual in this series:

   - Ask a student to describe the event or situation.
   - Discuss how this situation might affect people in other countries.
   - Ask students to list (on the handout L1, H1, page 146) jobs related to this event. Then make a master list on the board.
   - Lead a discussion on why it would be advantageous for people in jobs related to the environment to be able to understand other cultures' needs and views.
   - Describe environmental issues that relate to the specific language or culture being studied (e.g., Japan: whaling; Costa Rica: rain forest; France: nuclear testing; Bosnia: land mines).

2. Show the students items or visuals of items that are made or produced locally and exported to other countries. Go through the following sequence for each visual in this series:
   - Ask a student to describe the item or visual.
   - Discuss how these items affect the local economy.
   - Ask students to list (on the handout L1, H1, page 146) jobs that are influenced by international business, then make a master list.
   - Discuss with the class the advantages for people in jobs related to the economy to be able to understand the needs and views of other cultures.
   - Ask students to describe local, regional, or national products that are exported to the culture being studied (e.g., Japan: lumber, beef; Mexico: appliances, technology).
3. Show students pictures of current events related to world peace (covers of newsmagazines work well).
   - Ask students to describe the events.
   - Discuss how these events affect world peace.
   - Ask students to list jobs (on the handout L1, H1, page 146) that are influenced by these events.
   - Lead a discussion on the necessity for people in jobs related to world peace to be able to understand the needs and views of other cultures.
   - Describe the studied culture's role in international peacekeeping efforts.
4. Discuss with students the fact that in order to strive for a healthy environment, a productive economy, and lasting world peace we must understand the cultures of the people involved, and to truly understand a culture, one must learn the language. We are *interdependent* in these three areas. Our economy depends on other nations buying our goods; our country's peace depends on peace in other parts of the world; and our planet's health depends on people working together toward common goals.

   Finally, ask students to return to the question they answered at the beginning of the lesson and ask them if anyone would answer the question differently now. Discuss whether language and culture learning are luxuries or necessities. Ask students to brainstorm additional reasons (other than employment) for studying languages and cultures and write the group's responses in the last section (Other Benefits) of the handout.

Lesson 1—Follow-up Activity
Interdependence: A Complicated Web of Connections[2]

Introduction

Students need to view the world as many interdependent systems functioning together. This short follow-up lesson is meant to help them better understand the concept of *interdependence.*

Objective: Students will

- give concrete examples of interdependent systems and relate interdependency to the importance of learning other languages and cultures

Materials

- Ball of string/yarn
- Country cards. Print (large and bold) the following country names on paper or card stock, one country per paper: Korea, the United States, Ecuador, Colombia, Indonesia, China, Italy, Taiwan, France, Chile, Japan, Saudi Arabia, Brazil, Thailand.

Time: 20 minutes

Procedure

Part 1: Interdependent Systems

1. Have students brainstorm the types of jobs held by persons to help ensure quality patient care at a hospital. List them on the board. Then discuss the goods and services provided by the various employees. Possible answers include
   - administrative staff
   - food service
   - nurses
   - housekeeping services
   - doctors
   - pharmacists, etc.
2. Ask students to name other individuals, companies, or agencies who provide goods and services necessary for the hospital to function but who are not employees of the hospital. Possible examples include
   - research scientists
   - electric company
   - volunteers
   - telephone services
   - food suppliers, etc.

---

[2] Based in part on Pat Weiss, ed., *Kansas in the World* (Lawrence, KS: University of Kansas, 1991).

3. Discuss the concept of interdependence. From the hospital model, we can see that all health care professionals, support staff, and outside agencies must work together to provide care for patients.

   (Optional) Have students list other systems that are interdependent.

Part 2: Interdependent Nations

1. Discuss our dependence on other nations and other nations' dependence on us for goods and services to maintain and/or improve the standard of living.

   To illustrate the point, assign various students in the class to represent countries. Give them the respective country cards to hold. Slowly tell the story of John Doe, middle-class, middle-American citizen (see below). As you mention the first product, toss the ball of string to the student with the appropriate country card. That student tosses the ball of string (holding on to the string) to the next "country" mentioned, eventually forming a web which represents our dependency on other nations.

John Doe—A Web of Connections

*John Doe's alarm clock (**Korea**) went off this morning at 6:30 A.M. Mr. Doe got up and ate a breakfast consisting of cereal and milk (**USA**), a banana (**Ecuador**), grapefruit (**Chile**), and coffee (**Colombia**). He dressed in slacks from **Indonesia**, a shirt from **China**, shoes from **Italy**, and a tie from **France**. He listened to his radio (**Taiwan**) as he got ready for work. He threw his briefcase (**Brazil**) in his car (**Japan**) and drove (with gasoline from **Saudi Arabia** and tires made of rubber from **Thailand**) to work.*

2. Have students define *interdependency* in their own words and ask them to relate interdependency to the importance of foreign language and culture study.
3. (Optional) An extended activity could include a similar web for various products and materials that the students have used that day. This could be assigned as a homework activity.

Evaluation: Within one week of lesson 1 (and after the follow-up activity), ask students to respond to the questions below.

1. Why is learning a second language important to
   a. the economy of the United States?
   b. the environment of the United States and the world?
   c. world peace?
2. In what ways are countries dependent on each other?
3. What reasons might you personally have to learn a second or foreign language?

Student Handout (L1, H1)

Why Learn a Second or Foreign Language?

Environment: List jobs associated with nuclear energy and weapons, pollution control, endangered species, or the consequences of deforestation.

____

____

____

Economy: List jobs associated with international business.

____

____

____

World Peace: List jobs associated with world peace.

____

____

____

Other Benefits: Knowing another language and its cultures has benefits beyond increased employment possibilities. Name some of them.

____

____

____

Lesson 2–What Is Culture?

Introduction

Few students at the middle school level have a clear understanding of the concept of culture. Part of the reason for this is that culture means different things to different people. For these lessons, we will be using the general definition developed by cultural anthropologists: culture is the knowledge, skills, and values that shape an individual's ability to get along in his or her physical and social environment (Inkeles 1969). The concept of culture, because it is so broad, must utilize generalizations, which can lead to stereotypes. To avoid this, stress the fact that there will always be individual differences and exceptions among the members of a culture, alternate ways of looking at or doing things.

Samovar and Porter (1994), in their excellent introductory article on intercultural communication, define culture as

> *the deposit of knowledge, experience, beliefs, values, attitudes, meanings, hierarchies, religion, notions of time, roles, spatial relations, concepts of the universe, and material objects and possessions acquired by a group of people in the course of generations through individual and group striving (11).*

They also discuss three general categories of culture: artifacts—products of the group; concepts—values, beliefs, ways of knowing, and so forth of the group; and behaviors—the practice of the concepts mentioned above.[3]

Samovar and Porter propose six basic characteristics of culture.

1. Culture is not innate; it is learned.
2. Culture is transmissible (we teach it to our children verbally and nonverbally, explicitly and implicitly).
3. Culture is dynamic (it is subject to change).
4. Culture is selective (it chooses and defines the boundaries of the group).
5. Facets of culture are interrelated (a change in one aspect of culture may bring about changes in other aspects).
6. Culture is ethnocentric, centered on its own ways of being and seeing the world.

It is important that teachers recognize and teach the complex and interrelated nature of culture. Most experts agree that this can best be done by learning first about one's own cultural influences and boundaries.

---

[3] Traditionally, language teachers have focused their students' culture study on the artifact category of culture. Many language students have learned about a culture's history, fine arts, and literature, often referred to as "big C" culture. However, knowledge about historical times and great artists is just one way of increasing one's intercultural communication skills. We must also increase the focus on "little c" culture, studying both values and behaviors of cultural groups.

Objective: Students will

- define culture
- differentiate between cultural and individual or reflex behaviors
- experience the challenge of learning about culture
- evaluate the importance of studying culture in the language classroom

Materials

- "YES" and "NO" examples on large cards (see below)
- Balsa wood airplane or other small object with at least four parts (Choose something that, when broken into its various parts, is difficult to identify. You will also need one paper bag for each part.)

Time: One full class period and one shorter segment the following week

Procedure
Part 1: What Is Culture?[4]

1. Tell the students that by the end of class they will have defined and described the concept of culture, which will be used throughout their language and culture study.

   Read the Concept Attainment Strategy (L2, R1, page 152) prior to class. This activity makes use of the strategy to help students discover some of the attributes of culture. Before the lesson make large-print cards for each of the examples on page 149 (hint: use card stock and laminate for future use).

   Divide the chalkboard into halves. At the top of one half write "YES" and on the other, "NO." Explain to the class that you will be showing simple statements that may or may not be examples of the concept being examined. Using the teacher's examples as models, the students are to decide whether each statement is an example of the concept (YES) or is not an example of the concept (NO). Write each statement in the correct column on the board. Discuss as necessary.

   Do not tell the students the name of the concept in advance. Elicit essential characteristcs of the concept. If they do not eventually name the concept, the teacher can do so at the end of the activity.

   Mix up the examples and show one to the class. Then tape it to the appropriate side of the board, depending on whether it is an example of a culture-bound behavior (YES) or is not (NO). After several examples have been placed on each side, ask students to look for characteristics of the YES examples. List student-generated characteristics on the board. Proceed to new examples, adding to or deleting from the list of characteristics as you go. Have students begin making educated guesses about

---

[4] This activity is from Corinne Mantle-Bromley, "Preparing Students for Meaningful Culture Learning," *Foreign Language Annals* 25 (1992): 117-27.

the placement of the examples, and discussing why they think each example is a YES or a NO. Continue this process until the students can define *culture* from their list of characteristics. Essential attributes or characteristics of the concept of culture that the students should eventually name in their definition are: that it is learned and shared by a group of people, it is *not* shared by all groups of people, and it is necessary to know these things if you want to fit in with the group. After a definition is agreed upon by you and the class, write it on the board, then have the students offer their own examples for both sides of the board.

2. Have students copy the definition in their class notes and tell them they will be held responsible for both remembering the definition of culture and being able to give examples of cultural behaviors.

   YES (examples of culture)

   - A high school diploma is very important.
   - Parents generally live with the eldest son.
   - It is considered rude to keep your hands in your pockets.
   - Medical doctors are valued members of the community.
   - Guests are rarely entertained at home; they are usually entertained at a local restaurant.
   - Direct eye contact is expected.
   - You must not begin eating until everyone is served.
   - You give carnations only when a loved one dies.
   - Lunch is served at school.

   NO (not examples of culture)

   - The family calls your grandfather "Pops."
   - Your favorite color is blue.
   - Charlie doesn't whistle very well.
   - Dogs are known to carry ticks and fleas.
   - No one in your family likes broccoli.
   - Your uncle is a farmer.
   - Your favorite class is algebra.
   - You flinch when someone pretends to hit you in the face.
   - Your baby sister cries when she is hungry.

Part 2: Culture-Learning Experiment

1. (Before class, place each part from a balsa wood airplane model or other small object into a separate paper bag. Number the bags consecutively, with 1 as the most difficult piece from which to identify the whole item.[5])

   Tell the students they are going to conduct an experiment similar to trying to learn about another culture group or the culture of another country.

   One at a time, have several students reach into bag #1 without looking and describe what they feel. Ask them to guess what the piece belongs to.

   Continue this for several bags, having different students try to guess what the item is. Ask the students at various points why it is so difficult to determine the item. When they voice frustration, ask them why the exercise is frustrating. If students guess the item early, don't tell them until the end of the activity that they are correct.

   Continue until most of the bags have been explored. Have students continue guessing and describing their feelings.

   Depending on the maturity of your group, either explain or ask the students to explain how this activity is like learning another culture. We often only sense one manifestation of a culture and have to guess its meaning. Rarely do we see or feel all aspects of the cultural behavior at once. Similar feelings of frustration, like those experienced during the activity, are often present when something is happening within another culture that we do not understand. We have to continue gathering information and making informed guesses as to the cultural meaning.

   - Ask students to reflect on how the exercise relates to defining culture.
   - Have students redefine *culture*.
   - Ask for examples of American cultural behavior.
   - Ask for examples of individual behavior.
   - Ask why culture learning can be frustrating.

   Lead a discussion of why it is important to learn about culture in the class they are currently taking.

---

[5] This activity can be very successful. Critical to its success, however, is choosing an object that students don't often take apart. If the object is something that students don't recognize even when they see all of the parts, use this to suggest the difficulty of learning another culture. Even when we see all of the elements of a facet of the culture, we may still not understand it.

Lesson 2—Follow-up Activity
Exploring Cultures Close to Home

Introduction

Why learn about other cultures? Students should have a basic understanding of what culture is, but they still may not understand how important cultural understanding is in a variety of contexts. This short activity will allow them to explore the importance of cultural understanding close to home.

Objective: Students will

- explain to each other and to the teacher the role that cultural understanding plays in communicating in local cultures (and thereby extrapolate to people in other groups or country cultures)

Materials: None

Time: 25 minutes

Procedure

1. Ask the class to list behaviors that are expected in the school library (describe both student and librarian behaviors) or another local culture, such as a church, football game, school dance, and so forth. Ask students if this is cultural behavior and help them to see that it is learned behavior that helps people get along.

   Ask students what would happen if an international student came into a library without understanding American "library culture." Discuss how inappropriate behavior is handled in the library. Help students see that it is possible to learn the language but not learn the culture. Discuss the consequences of having language skills without cultural understanding. (You may have students role-play inappropriate library behavior.) Discuss personal examples of problems resulting from cultural misunderstandings.

Evaluation: Within one week of lesson 2 (and after the follow-up activity), ask students to answer the following questions.

1. What is culture?
2. What is an example of a cultural behavior?
3. Why do you think it is important to learn about a group's culture(s) as you learn the language?

Background Reading (L2, R1)

Concept Attainment Strategy[6]

When to Use It: When you want students to discover the essential attributes of a concept.

How to Use It

1. Select a concept and identify its essential attributes.
2. Organize material into positive and negative examples.
3. Scramble the examples and present them to students one by one, asking students to choose "Yes" (it is an example of the concept) or "No" (it isn't).
4. Have students identify the concept according to its essential attributes.
5. Ask students to generate additional examples of the concept.

How to Evaluate It

1. Are students able to describe the process they used to arrive at the essential attributes?
2. Are students able to identify the essential attributes?
3. Are students able to generate their own examples?

Things to Remember

1. Each positive example contains all of the essential attributes and values of the concept.
2. Arrange examples so that students can distinguish the essential attributes from the nonessential attributes in both negative and positive examples.

[6] See Bruce Joyce, Marsha Weil, and Beverly Showers, *Models of Teaching* (Boston: Allyn & Bacon, 1992).

Lesson 3—Stereotypes as Blocks to Second Language and Culture Learning

Introduction

Few students have had extensive contact with people from other cultures. Many, however, have formed definite ideas about what people from other cultures are like. In a study conducted in the Midwest (Mantle-Bromley 1994), middle school students were asked to write words and images they associated with various nationalities. For Germans, the students wrote primarily about World War II images (specifically references to Nazis) and the Berlin Wall. Students could not distinguish between people from Spain and people from Mexico. For example, when writing words and images they associated with Mexico and Mexicans, the students usually copied the words from the earlier Spanish nationality associations (tacos, burritos, nachos, dark skin and hair, poverty, and party images). Students most often associated fashion and romance with people from France. These stereotyped images will likely affect choice of language study, willingness to take on cultural behaviors such as pronunciation, and persistence in continuing to study the language.

Students' stereotypical ideas are based in large part on impressions gained from the media and on the beliefs of their parents, peers, and community. While some students will be familiar with stereotyping, and a few will be aware that they do it themselves, most will not have thought about how stereotypes originate and are perpetuated.

Negative feelings generated by stereotypes about another culture can affect a student's motivation to learn its language and culture(s). And, as we have seen, motivation is directly related to successful second language acquisition.

This lesson is based on the belief that the first step to eliminating stereotypes is recognizing that they exist and realizing their potentially harmful effects.

Objective: Students will

- define and give examples of stereotypes
- recognize the potentially harmful effects of accepting stereotypes
- identify examples of how our society maintains its stereotypes

Materials: Materials are described here for Japanese and Spanish classes. Teachers of other languages/cultures will need to find materials appropriate to their content areas.

- Teacher background reading on U.S./Japanese (U.S./Latino) stereotypes (L3, R1, pages 160–61 and L3, R2, page 162)
- Transparency of a stereotyped depiction of a Japanese (Latino) cartoon, caricature, etc. (L3, M1, page 163 and L3, M2, page 164)

- A series of ten to fifteen slides or pictures of Japanese (Latino) people in all walks of life, at all ages. Choose slides that will counter the narrow portrayal of the Japanese (Latino) in the media.[7]
- Evaluation quiz (L3, H1, page 159)

Time: One full class period and two ten-minute segments the following week, one for the follow-up activity, one for the evaluation quiz

Procedure

Part 1: Stereotypes via Soap Operas

1. Ask students if they have watched any soap operas on television, and have one or two of them describe some of the things that have happened.

   Explain that many of the most popular American soap operas are translated into other languages and are broadcast around the world. In fact, American television shows are common sources of information and are often used to determine what we in the United States are like.

   Have students generate a list of qualities that are common among the main characters in these shows; for example, rich, selfish, beautiful (handsome), lots of lovers, self-centered, and so on.

   Write the students' responses on the board.

2. Ask students if they know of anyone in real life who fits all of these characteristics or if they accurately describe the majority of Americans. Help students understand that beliefs about groups of people are formed, very often, from too little information.
3. Ask students what the harmful effects might be if large numbers of people thought that soap opera characters were typical of the majority of Americans. Some possible answers may include the following:
   - If people think we are all rich, they'll think we can give them aid whenever they need it.
   - If people think we are dishonest, they'll never trust us.

Part 2: Stereotypes of Student Groups

1. Ask students to name some of the cliques or groups within the school social structure (cheerleaders, athletes, etc.) and list the characteristics that students in each of these groups are commonly thought to have (stress that they aren't necessarily true, they are just common perceptions). Tell students that these are all examples of stereotypes, overgeneralized beliefs about what people are like based on the groups they are in, not on their individual personal characteristics.

---

[7] A wide variety of culture-related slides can be ordered from the Social Science Education Consortium, 3300 Mitchell Lane, Suite 240, Boulder, CO 80301-2272.

2. Ask students who belong to one of these groups to describe how it feels to be stereotyped or categorized in that way. Ask them what the danger of these beliefs is. Discuss with them the degree to which we all categorize other people and treat them according to our stereotypes of them, stereotypes based on too little knowledge and too much generalization.

Part 3: Stereotypes of the Target Culture

1. Now address the issue of stereotypes related to the target language and culture. Ask the students to name the characteristics that are commonly associated with the target culture and list them on the chalkboard. Some of these may be quite negative. Indicate that your intent is to see if together you can determine their validity.

   Discuss where these beliefs originated. For example, some beliefs about the Japanese are left over from World War II, when Americans were fighting the Japanese. It is known that during times of war, a culture will "demonize" the other culture in order to destroy it. Other beliefs about the Japanese have resulted from Japan's rapid rise in economic power. Beliefs about the German culture can also be traced to World War II and the Nazi movement. Common beliefs about the French are based, in part, on the high-profile export of beauty products to the United States.

   Help students examine the characteristics listed on the chalkboard. Try to determine, as a group, how the beliefs originated. Ask students how these stereotypes may actually damage cultural relations.

2. Show students via a transparency an example of a stereotype of the target culture. Discuss the media's role in perpetuating stereotypes.

   Next, instruct students to observe carefully the series of slides of Japanese (Spanish) speakers. Ask the students to write down as much detail about each slide as possible. Show the slides at about twenty- to thirty-second intervals.

   Have the students identify from what they saw on the slides characteristics consistent with the stereotype list on the board.[8] Then have them identify characteristics inconsistent with the stereotypes. Show the slides again if necessary.

   Draw the students' attention particularly to how little stereotypes may be based on fact.

---

[8] Based, in part, on J. Doyle Casteel and Miriam Williford, "Planning Cross-Cultural Lessons: Specifications for Design of Thirty-Three Learning Activities," Latin American Studies Association, 1976. (EDRS: ED 129 679).

Part 4: Defining Stereotype

1. Have students agree on a definition of *stereotype* that can then be recorded in their class notes.

Part 5: Independent Assignment

1. Ask students to look for and write down five examples of ways that our society maintains cultural stereotypes; for example, food packages, pictures in magazines, and scenes from television and movies are all possible sources. Students will share their examples with the class.

Lesson 3—Follow-up Activity
Identifying Stereotyped Behavior

Introduction

This activity will allow the teacher to check on individual students' understanding of stereotypes and clear up any confusion they have.

Objective: Students will

- analyze different scenarios and identify those which contain stereotyped thinking

Materials: Scenarios (below)

Time: 10 minutes

Procedure

1. Ask a student to put the group definition of *stereotype* on the board. Discuss some of the examples of stereotyped thinking that the students have brought to the class.
2. Read the following scenarios and have the students indicate whether or not they are examples of stereotyped thinking: thumbs up for "yes," thumbs down for "no." Discuss each example (answers are in italics).

Scenarios

- You have noticed that the store clerk at a particular store follows you and your friends around. You can tell that he thinks you might shoplift. *(Yes, the clerk is obviously treating you based on his stereotype of the "teenager" group to which you belong.)*
- There is a new student in your art class. She appears to be Mexican. You don't talk to her because you think she probably doesn't speak English very well. *(Yes, you think that because of her looks. You won't know if she speaks English until you talk with her.)*
- You have noticed that your piano teacher really likes the color purple and that she often wears scarves. For Christmas you buy her a purple scarf. *(No, this gift is based on personal knowledge of the teacher.)*
- Your older sister has the opportunity to go to Japan with a Japanese girl from her university. She decides not to go because she has heard that most Japanese believe Americans are lazy and stupid. *(Yes, she is basing her decision on what she has heard about Japanese people as a group. This will not be true about all Japanese.)*
- You've been invited to a friend's party. Your mother is surprised that you're not getting more dressed up for the party. You explain to her that everyone will be dressed similarly. (*No, you're making a decision based*

on personal knowledge of your friends.)

- Your father returns from an appointment with a medical surgeon. Both he and your mother are surprised that the surgeon is female. Although her credentials are very good, they're not quite comfortable having her perform an operation on your father. (*Yes, the parents in this case have created a stereotyped version of an ideal surgeon. Since this surgeon doesn't fit their picture, they're not sure the doctor will be good.*)

Evaluation: Within one week of the main lesson (and after the follow-up activity), ask students to complete the evaluation quiz (L3, H1, page 159).

Student Handout (L3, H1)

Evaluation Quiz

1. Some of the following descriptions are examples of stereotyped thinking and some are not. Put an X in the blanks to the left of those descriptions you believe *are* examples of stereotyped thinking.

____ a. The algebra teacher never calls on the football players in class because he believes that they aren't smart enough to know the correct answers.

____ b. Sara refuses to go on a date with Tom. She has watched him in math class and doesn't like the way he treats other girls in the class.

____ c. You go to the grocery store with your uncle. You notice that he speaks very slowly to the checkout girl (who appears to be Mexican American). Not only does he speak very slowly, but he also speaks louder. He thinks that she doesn't speak English well.

____ d. John goes to Japan with his parents over Christmas vacation. He is shocked to see people dressed in clothes similar to clothes in this country. He expected everyone to wear kimonos and sandals.

____ e. Your best friend's mother has asked you to their house for dinner. She fixes spaghetti and garlic bread because your friend told her that spaghetti is your favorite food.

____ f. Your elderly neighbor refuses to answer the door if a person of color (Hispanic, African American, etc.) rings the doorbell. She is afraid that the person will rob her.

____ g. You're surprised when you see the guest speaker for Spanish class. He has red hair, freckles, and blue eyes. You expected someone with darker features.

____ h. You friend's name is Johnny Lopez. Johnny couldn't understand why his teacher thought Johnny should know what the Mexican food *tamale* was. Johnny had no idea what this was.

____ i. You have purchased a beautiful vase for your mother. You have known she wanted it since you saw her circle it in a catalogue.

____ j. Your brother's football coach has been encouraging your brother, Tom, to play football in college. The coach thinks Tom is good enough to get a scholarship.

2. What is a stereotype?
3. What is the harm of stereotyped thinking?

Background Reading (L3, R1)

Stereotyped Japan

Americans on Japan: It's A Love-Hate Thing

Saatchi Study Finds U.S. Consumers Have Mixed Feelings About Japanese

By Cecilia Capuzzi Simon

NEW YORK—When it comes to their feelings about the Japanese, Americans are clearly a confused bunch.

A new study, commissioned by Saatchi & Saatchi, says an overwhelming majority of Americans believe Japanese industry and government are committed to dominating the world economy. The study also finds that Americans are "adamantly opposed" to increased Japanese acquisitions and investments in the U.S.

At the same time, though, Americans have no trouble spending their dollars on Japanese goods. They perceive the "Made in Japan" label as a sign of quality. In fact, half of those surveyed say they've purchased at least one Japanese item in the last four years.

A worldwide advertising agency with many Japanese clients, Saatchi & Saatchi says it is "concerned with the growing conflict over the relationship of Japan and the United States as partners in today's economy." It also fears the situation could "develop into business problems for our clients that are counterproductive and potentially destructive."

That's why the agency decided to undertake the far-reaching study, entitled *America and Japan In Conflict: An Emotional and Cultural Explanation.*

Saatchi hired Yankelovich Clancy Shulman to conduct the survey, and the company polled 800 Americans—including business, government and media leaders—for the two-part study.

The first section of the study is a survey of U.S. attitudes toward Japan. The second is an analysis of those findings and of Japanese-American relations by a team of clinical psychologists and cultural anthropologists.

Foremost among the survey's findings: Even 50 years after the Japanese bombing of Pearl Harbor, the U.S. and Japan still have quite a few differences to work out.

Americans harbor "ambivalent" feelings toward the Japanese, the study says. For example, while Americans see the Japanese as hard-working, loyal employees, they also believe them to be "crafty," "ill-intentioned," and unwilling to play fairly when it comes to righting the trade deficit.

STOP ME BEFORE I BUY AGAIN

Percentage of Americans who favor federal regulations that would severely limit importation of Japanese products into the U.S.	Percentage of Americans who say they refuse to buy Japanese products	Percentage of Americans who say they've bought big-ticket Japanese consumer goods within the past four years
59%	13%	49%

Source: Saatchi & Saatchi study, "America and Japan in Conflict: An Emotional and Cultural Explanation."

Saatchi explains this paradox by suggesting the U.S. is insecure. "Regardless of the recent developments in the Persian Gulf," the study says, "our key emotional needs as Americans are not being met as well as they once were." America sees itself, in the words of one respondent, as "an eagle with ruffled feathers."

The study also says that Americans feel "vulnerable" and have low self-esteem. Therefore they are in need of a "scapegoat to channel [their] negative feelings into."

And, because Americans perceive the Japanese as "separate, ill-intentioned and superior," they vent their frustrations at them. As the study points out, Britain and the Netherlands own as large a share of American businesses as the Japanese. But because the English and the Dutch look similar to Americans, Americans don't believe them to be superior. Therefore, they are no threat.

There's no doubt that the imperial Japanese hold different values from the self-made Yankee. Americans, says Saatchi, believe in the "ethic of individual effort.... In the eyes of Americans, a fair society is based on the win-or-lose stance of freely competing individuals." The study also says Americans are often considered "too forward or too frank by other cultures."

The Japanese, on the other hand, value "commitment to the group." This means, to sum up the explanation of the anthropologists and psychologists who analyzed the findings, that Americans view their competitors across the Pacific as regimented, uncreative, ingenuine and boring. They also resent Japanese restraints on trade.

What's to be done? Saatchi says Americans and Japanese have to be made to realize that they have much in common. For example, the study asserts, both nations share the "ideal of a prosperous society achieved by hard work." Americans, after all, are repenting the grabby, affluent ways of the '80s while excoriating such icons as Donald Trump, Michael Milken and savings and loan executives.

The study leaves out some interesting points, however. Nowhere, for instance, does the study suggest that Americans could regain their self-respect and that the U.S. could recapture the domestic and world market by improving its educational system.

It also neglects to mention the material and mental benefits Americans stand to gain if they begin producing a greater number of high-quality products that are capable of challenging the Japanese in the global marketplace. ■

MEETING HALFWAY

What can be done to bridge the gap between American and Japanese cultures? The new Saatchi & Saatchi study makes several suggestions. "The differences in values...needs to be recognized and accepted," the study says.

Saatchi suggests that Japanese corporations must address those differences and help foster a kind of cultural respect. Other suggestions aimed at Japanese companies include "Establishing joint ventures that require U.S. companies' expertise and involvement; highlighting American technology in Japanese products; giving credit to American ingenuity and know-how; and demonstrating that the Japanese are contributing to the well-being of America."

Background Reading (L3, R2)

Stereotyped Mexico

Crazy distinction in bias survey

by MARGARITA ENGLE

I usually have a fair amount of confidence in my ability to understand the English and Spanish languages, but recently I read an article that sent me scurrying for a stack of dictionaries.

"White people oppose racial discrimination more than

HISPANIC LINK

ever, but still cling to stereotypes of blacks and Latinos," the Associated Press reported, quoting a survey by the National Opinion Center.

"Three of four whites believe blacks and Latinos are more likely than whites to prefer living on welfare," the opinion poll found. "The majority of whites also believe blacks and Latinos are more likely than whites to be lazy, violence-prone, less intelligent and less patriotic."

These statistics paint a grim picture of ignorance, intolerance and plain, old-fashioned racism, racism in the sense of that dated but accurate word "prejudice."

Prejudice is defined by Webster's New Dictionary as "a judgment or opinion formed before the facts are known."

Can a person believe a stereotype without being prejudiced? Webster's defines "stereotype" as "an unvarying form or pattern...having no individuality, as though cast from a mold."

In other words, people who believe racial stereotypes such as "lazy," "prone-to-violence" and "less intelligent" have formed opinions about their neighbors before the facts are known.

The facts, of course, can be known only on an individual basis. Knowing that one man named "Joe" is prone to violence won't tell you whether all men named Joe are dangerous.

Equally troubling is the acceptance of stereotypes by blacks and Latinos. In the survey, 5.1 percent of Latinos rated themselves less intelligent than whites.

Did the Latinos really understand that they were rating themselves less intelligent? Or did they think they were stating that Latinos are less likely to be educated?

The difference between intelligence and education is like the difference between earthquakes and dynamite. Earthquakes are unpredictable; but if you light a stick of dynamite, chances are you'll get an explosion.

Appleton's New Cuyas Spanish-English Dictionary translates intelligence as *inteligencia, penetracion, sagacidad, conocimiento, informe, noticia, aviso.*

Some of the surveyed Latinos may have been completely fluent in English. Others may have had to do a little simultaneous translation in their minds as they considered each question.

Some may have heard *penetracion* (clearsightedness, or penetration), *sagacidad* (wisdom), *conocimiento* (knowledge), *informe* (information), *noticia* (news) or *aviso* (announcement).

Only the first translation would judge one's ability to learn. The rest refer to an explosion more likely to occur among those who've had access to the dynamite of education. My guess is many of the Latinos polled were hearing *conocimiento*, and were stating that Latinos were less likely to have accumulated as much knowledge since they were less likely to have completed school.

If I'm wrong, then the future for Latinos in the U.S. is bleak. Nothing is more damaging to a person's self-esteem and ambition than the internalization of negative stereotypes about himself.

Margarita Mondrus-Ferrer Engle, an agronomist living in Fallbrook, Calif., writes for literary and professional journals.

(L3, M1)

Stereotyped Japan

(L3, M2)

Stereotyped Mexico

Lesson 4—Ethnocentrism as a Block to Second Language and Culture Learning

Introduction

Students in their early to midteens place a great deal of importance on being like their peers and assign negative value to being different. This runs parallel to the basic human ethnocentric impulse to seek security through strong identification with one's group.

It is common to approve of those behaviors similar to one's own and to judge differences as somehow bad or wrong. This tendency to evaluate differences negatively inhibits students' abilities to accept differences as viable alternatives. For example, language students may view the correct pronunciation of the Spanish *rr* sound (or the French *r* or the German *g*) as stupid or unnecessary, since the sound does not exist in the English language. This ethnocentric belief may keep them from accepting and using correct pronunciation of the foreign language.

This lesson will lay the groundwork for helping students understand and deal with ethnocentric reactions that may emerge during the language learning process. After the lesson is completed, refer to it and to the concept of ethnocentrism whenever possible. As students react to linguistic or cultural differences in an ethnocentric manner, point out their behavior. Help them to see how strong this tendency is.

Objective: Students will

- experience the frustration that often accompanies trying to shift linguistic and/or cultural perspective
- define ethnocentrism
- recognize and give examples of ethnocentrism
- demonstrate empathic behavior

Materials

- Young/old woman transparency (L4, M1, page 169)
- Transparency of two women or two men embracing
- Transparency of students in their school uniforms

Time: One class period and one fifteen-minute segment the following week

Procedure

Part 1: Perception—the Young/Old Woman

1. Ask the students to describe to you what they see in the projected transparency (L4, M1, page 169). Some may see the withered old woman, others may see a very glamorous younger woman. For some, it will be hard to see both, even after students trace the parts of the face. Ask students why it is so difficult for some people to see both figures. *Once you have seen something one way it's hard to look at it*

another way.

2. Ask students how this exercise is related to learning about a new culture. How will this phenomenon of looking at something just one way limit our learning? What must we do if we are to learn as much as possible about other cultures?

Part 2: Ethnocentrism

1. Find a picture of two women or two men embracing. (You may need to ask another foreign language [French or Spanish] teacher for a picture from a textbook.) Enlarge the picture and make a transparency. Ask students to react to the picture. Most likely they will react negatively, particularly if the picture involves kissing. Don't say anything to the students, just observe their reactions. This exercise can also be done using a picture of a food not commonly consumed in the United States (e.g., fish heads) or other cultural artifacts or practices that will generate a negative response.

   Write *ethnocentrism* on the board. Tell the class you're going to give some examples, and they are going to try to determine what the word means by analyzing some examples. Take your examples from personal experiences, for example,

   - You eat pizza with your hands and think it is crazy to eat it with a fork.
   - You cut your meat with your fork in your left hand but switch your fork to the right hand to eat. People who do otherwise are weird.
   - Your friend Freddy's family doesn't eat dinner until 9:00 P.M. That is really crazy!

   Have students brainstorm a definition. Keep giving them examples until their definition is something like this: *ethnocentrism* is when a person believes his or her culture's way of doing something is right and other ways are wrong, illogical, or even immoral.

   After students have defined *ethnocentrism,* ask them for personal examples.

   Now return to the students' reactions of the two women or two men embracing. Ask students if some of their reactions were based on ethnocentrism. Have students explain why.

   Discuss with students the European custom of greeting friends with an embrace and one or two kisses on the cheek. Ask how ethnocentrism might get in the way of their learning the culture if they were to go to Europe. Ask what they might do to get over the feelings they associate with this behavior.

2. Show the class a transparency of a picture of students in school uniforms. (Ask the Spanish or Japanese teacher for pictures from a text-

book.) First, ask the students to look only for similarities between these students and themselves. List as many similarities as possible.

Next, state the obvious difference (uniforms). Discuss the idea of wearing uniforms to school. Help students to recognize any ethnocentric comments.

Ask students to picture themselves going to school with these students and wearing a uniform identical to theirs. Ask them to complete the following sentences on paper, pretending that they attended school with these students last year.[9] (Write these on the chalkboard.)

- I didn't mind wearing a uniform when ________________________ .
- Sometimes I hated wearing my uniform when ________________ .
- The good thing about uniforms is ___________________________ .

Discuss students' answers, encouraging those students who were able to put themselves in the place of the uniform-clad students.

Part 3: Conclusion

1. On the same sheet of paper the students just used, have them write down what they learned from the young/old woman picture related to culture learning.

   Next, have them write down what they learned from the transparencies of two men or two women embracing or of the students in school uniforms.

   Ask students to write down their own definition for *ethnocentrism* and as many examples of ethnocentric behavior as possible—as observed in their friends, the news media, TV shows, themselves.

2. Ask students to participate in the following experiment. Have them practice pronunciation of a short list of foreign words that (1) contain a sound not present in the English language and (2) are difficult for English speakers to pronounce correctly. Ask them to note and discuss any ethnocentric tendencies to evaluate the new sound as stupid or wrong.

   Discuss with students that ethnocentrism is a common reaction to differences. Even though there are several ways to view reality, we tend to see only one way. We then evaluate other ways negatively. Becoming aware of these tendencies is the first step to reducing ethnocentrism and accepting differences as alternatives to our own ways.

---

[9] From Gail L. Nemetz Robinson, *Cross-Cultural Understanding* (New York: Prentice-Hall, 1988).

Second, we can try to understand the new or different behavior by looking at it from a different perspective (shift our perspective) and trying to understand from the other person's point of view.

Evaluation: Within one week of lesson 4 have students write answers to the following questions.

1. Explain the relationship between perception and ethnocentrism and why ethnocentrism can make language and culture learning more difficult.
2. Write a definition of *ethnocentrism*.
3. Describe an ethnocentric belief or behavior.
4. Explain why ethnocentrism can make language and culture learning more difficult.

(L4, M1)

Lesson 5—Subcultures within Broader Cultures

Introduction

The previous lessons have focused on culture in general. However, students need to be reminded constantly of the importance of subcultures within broad cultural frameworks. There are many differences among any grouping of people. Oftentimes stereotypes are created by attributing characteristics of a subculture to everyone in the culture. For example, many people believe that all Mexican men wear large hats. This is true of most Mexican men who work as farmers or field-workers. It may not be true, however, of Mexican males who are doctors or plumbers or teachers.

If students understand that cultural characteristics may be accurately attributed only to a subculture rather than to everyone in the culture, they will be less likely to form stereotypes from what they learn in their language classes.

Objective: Students will

- define *subculture*
- recognize similarities and differences among various subcultures
- identify important features of "American" cultures
- determine topics within the target culture, that is, the culture of the language they are learning, that will be important for them to learn

Materials: None

Time: One full class period and one shorter segment the following week

Procedure

Part 1: Subcultures

1. Write "Similarities" on one side of the chalkboard and "Differences" on the other. Ask students to name another same-level school in their own or a neighboring district.[10] Remind students of the tendency to look at differences in a negative light (ethnocentrism) and the tendency to see the differences more than the similarities.

   Begin by having the students list similarities between the other school and their own, then differences. Record their comments on the board. Ask them to reflect on the positive and negative values inherent in both lists (usually students will rate differences negatively). Discuss possible reasons why we often see differences negatively: *It puts the way we do something in a more positive light; it is ethnocentric.*

[10] Based, in part, on Madeline A. Cooke, "Suggestions for Developing More Positive Attitudes toward Native Speakers of Spanish," in *Teaching Cultural Concepts in Spanish Classes,* edited by H. Ned Seelye (Springfield, IL: Office of the Superintendent of Public Instruction, 1972), 97-107.

2. Conduct the same activity comparing, for example, boys with girls, teenagers with adults, parents with grandparents, people from the east coast with people from the west coast.

   Now break the students into pairs and have them list similarities and differences between their families.

   Discuss the family similarities and differences with the entire class. In the same way that different families within one culture differ from each other, different subcultures within a culture vary considerably in some but not all characteristics.

   Point out to students that there are many patterns of differences *within a culture*. There will be numerous exceptions to any general cultural trait of a group of people. When a group within a culture demonstrates patterns that differ from the larger group or are in addition to patterns of the larger group, that group is classified as a subculture.

   Have students list various subcultures that exist within the American culture, for example,

   - ethnic groups (e.g., Hispanic Americans, African Americans)
   - age groups (e.g., teenagers, elderly)

3. Explain the following activity to the whole class, then break into groups of three or four to complete it.

   In small groups, brainstorm and write down as many possible elements as your group can think of that reflect or symbolize some particular aspect of American culture. (You may want to start out this activity as a whole group, then move to small groups for the next stage.) Ideas to get students started: Mickey Mouse, George Washington, shopping malls, Thanksgiving, grocery stores that have banks and pharmacists inside, and so forth.

   In the small groups, decide on the absolutely essential topics to include in a short course on American culture for teenage international students coming to the United States to live for a year. In other words, what would they need to know about American culture[11] that would help them adjust to our country?

   As a whole class, discuss the different groups' lists. How many items did every group have in common? Why is there such diversity in the groups?

   Tie the lesson back to subgroups. Have the students examine their lists to see if their topics apply to American culture in general or if they are specific to a particular subculture (e.g., teenagers). Would the list be different for Japanese businesspeople? Why?

---

[11] Based, in part, on Paula R. Heusinkveld, "The Foreign Language Classroom: A Forum for Understanding Cultural Stereotypes," *Foreign Language Annals* 18 (1985): 321-25.

4. Ask students to help design a course syllabus that would best prepare them to live with a family from the target culture for a year. First, determine what subgroups would be important to study. (For example, would it be important to study about specific professions? Specific age groups? Specific regional differences? Religious differences?) Then begin generating a list of topics within each subculture category. Finally, give students a realistic picture of how many of their ideas will be studied in their language class.

Evaluation: Culture is often approached as if it were one way of living/seeing the world. If students are to appreciate the subtleties of culture, they must begin seeing the numbers of factors influencing one's perspective. Have students answer the following questions.

1. Define *subculture*.
2. Explain why the elderly would be considered a subculture within the larger American culture.
3. List three elements of American teenage culture.
4. List three subcultures of the target culture that would be important to study before visiting the country.

Lesson 5—Follow-up Activity
Who Am I?

Introduction

Students will better understand various cultural influences on others if they can first understand cultural influences on themselves. This short activity is meant to help students recognize how various subcultural factors influence each of them.

Objective: Students will

- identify subcultural influences on their own identity

Materials: Paper, pencils, rulers

Time: 15 minutes

Procedure

1. Have students list the subcultures to which they belong that influence who they are and how they view the world, for example, "gender," "age group," "student." Then have them draw a pie chart that illustrates the various subculture categories and the relative importance of each category to their identity. The larger the influence is, the larger the "piece of pie" will be.

   Have students present their charts to each other, explaining specifically how one subculture category influences who they are.

Lesson 6–Observation versus Judgment

Introduction

From previous lessons, students have learned about stereotypes and ethnocentrism. Now they will learn how these two natural tendencies act as filters on our perceptions, causing premature (and usually negative) judgments about a person or even an entire culture.

Merriam Webster's Collegiate Dictionary, 10th ed., defines *fact* as the "quality of being actual." When students are asked to write down facts about an event, however, what they often put down is *perceived* information. For example, they may describe a fish market worker as being poor, happy, a lover of fish, and so on, without having verified those characteristics. Without training, we tend to make judgments about what we see, judgments that are biased by our own cultural experiences, that is, our ethnocentrism and, often, stereotypes. Once we perceive something or someone according to these judgments, it is very difficult to alter our perception. This lesson will provide practice on differentiating between observation and judgment and will offer students the opportunity to sharpen their observational skills about another culture while withholding judgment. Through practice of nonjudgmental observation, students can truly learn about other cultures.

Objective: Students will

- learn to differentiate between judgments and observations
- practice stating observations about people and places
- see similarities and differences between cultures with equal clarity

Materials

- At least six slides of the target culture that will likely elicit judgmental reactions. Japan-related slides might include foods not commonly eaten in the United States, a woman bowing deeply, or children serving lunch or cleaning the school bathrooms. Slides for the Spanish class might include pictures of native Indian people's dress or housing, foods not commonly eaten, or bullfighting.

Time: One full class period and one fifteen-minute segment the following week

Procedure

Part 1: Observation versus Judgment[12]

1. Instruct students to take out paper and a pencil. Then show them the first slide in your series. Ask students to individually write down five

[12] From Alvino E. Fantini, Mary V. McCoy, Julie Soquet, Elizabeth Tannenbaum, and Larraine Wright, *Cross-Cultural Orientation: A Guide for Leaders and Educators* (Brattleboro, VT: Experiment in International Living, 1984).

facts that they can observe about the picture (at this point, do not tell them what you mean by *facts*). When everyone is finished, ask students to volunteer their "facts" while you list them on the board.

Next, write "Observation" and "Judgment" on the board. With the help of the class and a dictionary if necessary, arrive at a definition for each word that the class and you can accept. Ask students if *facts* would be observations or judgments.

Ask students to determine which of the "facts" on the board are observations and which are judgments. Label each with a *J* or an *O*. Students will sometimes resist the judgment label. Help them see the difference between fact (objective description of what one sees) and judgment (what one feels about what one sees).

Discuss our tendency to make premature judgments when we do not have full information about a given person or situation. Also remind students of our ethnocentric tendency to look from our own perspective and judge according to our own culture.

Tell the students about the slide. Give students personal information, if possible.

Ask students to relate examples in their lives where premature judgments have been made before full information about the situation was available. Relate this to the activity with the model airplane and the paper bags (lesson 2). *It is difficult to determine the whole when only seeing or feeling one small part.*

Part 2: Looking for Similarities and Differences

1. Discuss with students the concept that while we may *see*, take note of, or observe differences through our senses more readily than we do similarities, in the *assumptions* we make about people and their cultures—their values, ways of thinking, and styles of communication—we are much more likely to assume similarities than differences. Some of the most basic differences may not be readily observable. Most people, for example, can't immediately observe differences between the British and Americans, therefore falsely assuming that the two peoples and cultures are very similar. They are not.

   Show several more slides. For each slide ask the students to identify as many similarities between the slide and their own culture as they can and state them in the form of observations rather than judgments.

   Now go back through the slides and ask the students to look for differences and again state them as observable facts. No judgments allowed! While viewing the slides a second time, explain to the students the background on each slide.

   It is possible that some of the students' comments will be ethnocentric. If this occurs, point it out. Don't scold them, just help them to see how easily we use our culture as the guide for what is right or logical.

Part 3: Conclusion

1. After erasing the board and asking students to cover their papers, call on individuals to summarize the lesson and to define *judgment* and *observation.* Ask why it is important to look for both similarities and differences.

Evaluation: This activity allows students to practice their new skill of nonjudgmental observation. Use the same procedure for the practice slide and the evaluation slide.

1. Show students a practice slide of the target culture and ask them to list on paper six facts about the picture. Put students' facts on the board and, as a group, label them as observations or judgments.
2. For the evaluation slide, omit the group discussion. Ask students to individually label each of their six facts with either *J* (judgment) or *O* (observation) and then pass in their papers for evaluation.

Annotated Bibliography

Bennett, Milton J. "Towards Ethnorelativism: A Developmental Model of Intercultural Sensitivity." In *Education for the Intercultural Experience*, edited by R. Michael Paige. Yarmouth, ME: Intercultural Press, 1993.

Casteel, J. Doyle, and Miriam Williford. "Planning Cross-Cultural Lessons: Specifications for Design of Thirty-Three Learning Activities." Latin American Studies Association, 1976. (EDRS: ED 129 679).

Cooke, Madeline A. "Suggestions for Developing More Positive Attitudes toward Native Speakers of Spanish." In *Teaching Cultural Concepts in Spanish Classes*, edited by H. Ned Seelye. Springfield, IL: Office of the Superintendent of Public Instruction, 1972.

Fantini, Alvino E., Mary V. McCoy, Julie Soquet, Elizabeth Tannenbaum, and Larraine Wright. *Cross-Cultural Orientation: A Guide for Leaders and Educators.* Brattleboro, VT: Experiment in International Living, 1984. An excellent resource for culture-learning exercises.

Gardner, Robert C. *Social Psychology and Second Language Learning: The Role of Attitudes and Motivation.* London: Arnold, 1985. A review of research.

Hanvey, Robert G. *An Attainable Global Perspective.* New York: New York Friends Group, Center for War/Peace Studies, 1975. (EDRS: ED 116 993). A description of culture-learning levels attainable in the language classroom.

Heusinkveld, Paula R. "The Foreign Language Classroom: A Forum for Understanding Cultural Stereotypes." *Foreign Language Annals* 18 (1985): 321-25. Lesson suggestions.

Inkeles, Alex. "Social Structure and Socialization." In *Handbook of Socialization Theory and Research*, edited by D. A. Goslin. Chicago: Rand McNally, 1969.

Joyce, Bruce, Marsha Weil, and Beverly Showers. *Models of Teaching.* Boston: Allyn & Bacon, 1992. Excellent description of concept attainment lessons.

Mantle-Bromley, Corinne. "Preparing Students for Meaningful Culture Learning." *Foreign Language Annals* 25 (1992): 117-27. Description of common attitudinal blocks to second language learning.

———. "Misconceptions and Cultural Stereotypes of Middle School Students Learning a Second Language." *Middle School Journal* 26 (1994): 42-47.

———. "Positive Attitudes and Realistic Beliefs: Links to Proficiency." *Modern Language Journal* 79 (1995): 372-86.

Mantle-Bromley, Corinne, and Raymond B. Miller. "Effect of Multicultural Lessons on Attitudes of Students of Spanish." *Modern Language Journal* 75 (1991): 418-25. Results of research on attitude change in the language class.

Robinson, Gail L. Nemetz. *Cross-Cultural Understanding.* New York: Prentice-Hall, 1988. Highly recommended for all second language teachers.

Samovar, Larry A., and Richard E. Porter. "An Introduction to Intercultural Communication." In *Intercultural Communication: A Reader,* 7th ed., edited by Larry A. Samovar and Richard E. Porter. Belmont, CA: Wadsworth, 1994.

Social Science Education Consortium, 3300 Mitchell Lane, Suite 240, Boulder, CO 80301-2272. (303) 492-8154. Excellent source for cultural slides of people and places from around the world.

Triandis, Harry C. *Attitude and Attitude Change.* New York: Wiley, 1971.

Weiss, Pat, ed. *Kansas in the World.* Lawrence: University of Kansas, 1991. A description of both global interdependence and lesson suggestions.

Wurzel, Jaime S. "Multiculturalism and Multicultural Education." In *Toward Multiculturalism: A Reader in Multicultural Education,* edited by Jaime S. Wurzel. Yarmouth, ME: Intercultural Press, 1988.